The Secrets of GLOBAL SALES

BUILD, NAVIGATE, AND ACCELERATE YOUR INTERNATIONAL GROWTH

WENDY MACKENZIE PEASE & HANNAH FELDMAN PENTZ

The Secrets of

GLOBAL SALES

BUILD, NAVIGATE, AND ACCELERATE YOUR INTERNATIONAL GROWTH

WENDY MACKENZIE **PEASE**
& HANNAH FELDMAN **PENTZ**

Ordering Information:
Special discounts are available on quantity purchases by corporations, associations, educational institutions, and others. For details, contact www.wendypease.com or wmpease@RapportTranslations.com, +1-978-443-2540

ISBN: 979-8-9925206-2-0

Tilt Publishing
700 Park Offices Drive, Suite 250
Research Triangle, NC 27709

DEDICATION

To David and Robert Pease—thank you for inspiring my growth!

To every export initiator, leader, manager, team member, marketer, vendor, advisor, cultural expert, consultant, financier, lawyer, logistician, supply chain specialist—thank you for keeping the journey fun!

—Wendy

To John—Thank you for your continued love and support along this journey.

To Jacob and George—I hope you continue to explore your passions as you experience the adventure of life.

—Hannah

TABLE OF CONTENTS

Introduction – Stories from Abroad

I. **Laying the Groundwork** **15**

    1. Think Global from the Start – *Omer Menashe* 17

    2. Don't Go Too Little, Too Slow – *Aytul Ercil* 23

    3. Don't Go Too Big, Too Fast – *Brittany Cooper Kingdon* 29

    4. Be Strategic – *Stephanie Hendricks* 35

    5. Research Drives Strategy and Mitigates Risk – *John Jove* 39

II. **Navigating Language and Culture** **47**

    6. Consolidate Your Global Message – *Michelle Safrit* 49

    7. Insider's Perspective on AI and Translation – *Adam Bittlingmayer* 55

    8. Conquer Cultural Issues – *Carole Copeland Thomas* 63

    9. Stay Curious and Make Connections – *Nick Canfield* 71

    10. Build Trust for International Sales – *Zach Selch* 77

III. **Fueling Growth from Within** **83**

    11. Use Local Employees Wisely – *Randi Roger* 85

    12. It Takes a Vision – *Andrew Jason* 91

    13. Multinational vs. Global Marketing – *Liz Fendt* 97

IV. Driving Growth **101**

   14. Unleashing the Potential of Trade Shows – *Walter Brooks* 103

   15. Leveraging LinkedIn – *Viveka von Rosen and AJ Wilcox* 111

   16. Connecting with People – *Babs Ryan* 119

   17. Building Global Communities – *Dani Weinstein* 125

V. Taking the Leap **131**

   18. Starting... – *Ed Marsh* 133

   19. Moving Gracefully from Localized to Globalized – *Patrick Nunes* ... 137

   20. Helpful Resources Are Available – *Wendy Pease* 143

   21. Success Is Attainable! 149

   22. Bonus Materials and Special Offers 151

Endnotes **155**

Acknowledgments **157**

About the Authors **159**

INTRODUCTION

STORIES FROM ABROAD

"Exporting can be profitable for businesses of all sizes. On average, sales grow faster, more jobs are created, and employees earn more than in non-exporting firms."

—*US International Trade Office website*[1]

W alter Brooks first learned about the lack of real competition for Southern-style barbeque (BBQ) in Saudi Arabia while at a local food show in Atlanta, Georgia. A chance encounter with an export representative turned out to be a fortuitous meeting.

"There's a BBQ sauce maker on every corner in Atlanta, so my competition was rough," he explained on the *Global Marketing Show*. Yet once he began exporting his product internationally, Walter's company revenue exploded in growth: from zero to $10 million in two years.

How did he manage such enormous growth, and so quickly? To understand, we must examine his unique story. and many others, as we explore the secrets of global sales.

RESOURCES FOR EXPORTERS

There are many opportunities and tricks to access international markets, which most people do not recognize or are afraid to tap into. Walter didn't set out to export when beginning his business as, he didn't realize there was an international demand. Yet when approached by a trade rep offering knowledge, funds, and support services, he couldn't resist the opportunity.

The international export market offers enormous potential for United States of America (US) based companies. In fact, according to the US Department of Commerce's research, only 173,459 exporters are responsible for $1,322.2 billion in revenue.[2] That is a lot of revenue spread among a relatively small number of companies!

Despite this, exporting is not only for large companies. According to the office of the United States Trade Representative (USTR), "Small businesses which export grow faster, add jobs faster, and pay higher wages, accounting for 98 percent of all identified US exporters and supporting nearly four million jobs in communities across America** through both direct and indirect exports."[3]

Federal and state export representatives work with small and midsized companies all over the US to make introductions to potential international partners, increase exporting, provide grants for activities (like translation), and offer advice on exporting – just like they did for Walter. Yet many business owners are unaware of these programs because, rather than spending their budgets on advertising these services, the export offices allocate their funds to support export activities of participating companies.

THE BIRTH OF AN IDEA

After writing *The Language of Global Marketing*, a "how-to" book for business leaders who want to grow their international sales and marketing, we heard from many readers who wanted more real-life examples. One way we share these stories is on our podcast the *Global Marketing Show*. Through the podcast, we encourage growing organizations to learn from others how to access new markets and achieve the exponential growth that exporters experience.

Armed with these amazing stories we began compiling some of the most pertinent lessons to inspire and guide others in their global sales journey.

** *Please note that throughout the chapters, although we use the term "American" to refer to people living in the US, we certainly do not mean to offend those living in Central or South America, or Canada. It is just a simple way to use a recognized term to refer to a group of people.*

For example, along with learning about how Walter Brooks worked with a trade rep and grew his small BBQ sauce company (Chapter 14), we also included stories about:

- Building a growth strategy and consolidating global messaging
- Finding the sweet spot for growth – not too fast or too slow
- Leveraging less expensive advertising on LinkedIn for global exposure
- Using (or not using) artificial intelligence and automation for your translation

We worked hard to choose the most insightful information from the podcast episodes to offer options not often considered, and to highlight the resources available.

EVERY STORY IS UNIQUE

These real-life stories from entrepreneurs, global marketing experts, and CEOs remind us that each person's and each company's journey is unique, yet they all have a compelling story to share. Some of the conversations on the podcasts were lively and full of laughter as we recalled mistakes and cultural gaffes. In others, the guests recounted specific steps that they took for expansion.

Even though some of the guests moved to new roles since we recorded the podcast and before we went to print, we included their stories to share their pearls of timeless wisdom. We chose the episodes to highlight stories with practical, inspirational, and actionable advice for exporting.

ADDITIONAL RESOURCES AND LEARNING

As you read, you may be interested in hearing the person speak directly about their experiences. All original episodes can be heard on the *Global Marketing Show* website[4] or on any of your favorite podcast listening apps (just search "*Global Marketing Show*"). Additionally, we provide a link to each specific episode so you can hear the full episode and access links to resources the guests recommend.

 The final chapter provides a link for you to access Bonus Materials (🎁) that are free to readers. These materials include things like:

- Links to finding federal and state offices that help companies export

- Free supporting materials for new exporters, such as an Exporting Treasure Map and Global Marketing email mini-course

- Further reading options on a variety of topics relating to global marketing

- And more…

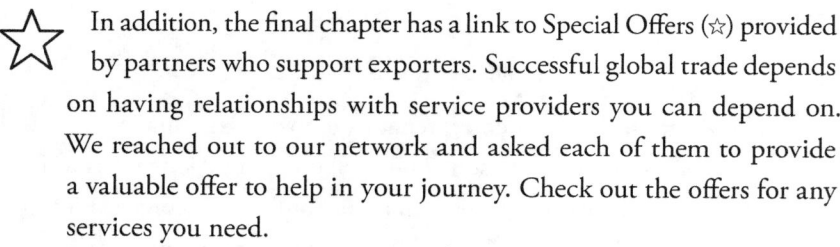 In addition, the final chapter has a link to Special Offers (☆) provided by partners who support exporters. Successful global trade depends on having relationships with service providers you can depend on. We reached out to our network and asked each of them to provide a valuable offer to help in your journey. Check out the offers for any services you need.

Our hope is that these stories help you realize the amazing potential of exporting your goods or services, enabling you to increase your company's growth dramatically.

KEEP Growing!

Wendy MacKenzie Pease and Hannah Feldman Pentz

LAYING THE GROUNDWORK

CHAPTER 1

THINK GLOBAL FROM THE START

"To increase your understanding, step outside of your own expectations."

—*Omer Menashe, Lightway Digital, CEO*

A s you read through these stories, you will notice a recurring theme: "Think global from the start." In the Introduction, we mentioned the enormous sales revenue that a relatively small number of exporters bring into the US. Unfortunately, in larger countries like the US, entrepreneurs don't always start out with a global mindset.

Organizations based in larger countries have the perceived luxury of not needing to export. They believe the home market offers unending sales opportunities. Yet, eventually smart leaders realize that global audiences want their products and international markets offer huge opportunities.

Initially in their expansion efforts, organizations often show an inherent bias toward their home culture. Products and services lack adaptation for globalization, and the company culture and marketing initiatives struggle to adapt for international audiences.

In a small country, however, an organization must think globally from the start, since its domestic market will not support enough growth to reach minimal financial goals. Although this appears difficult at first, it gives the organization an advantage of preparing for global growth much earlier.

Omer Menashe, CEO of the Israeli-based digital marketing ad agency Lightway Digital[5], describes his experience in his podcast interview on the *Global Marketing Show* (Episode 67). In Israel, if investors think that your startup has too much Israeli concentration, they will avoid you: "It is not unusual for investors to try to get you to shy away from focusing on Israel because they want you to go elsewhere. They don't want you to have too much traction at home." As a result, companies focus on international markets early on, which leads to a better chance of success.

While investors in larger countries are less likely to encourage exports, it's still good business sense for a US-based startup to think globally from the start. Statistics from the US Department of Commerce show that US exporters have, on average, 20% greater revenue than their domestic counterparts. Moreover, they are more likely to stay in business, pay higher wages, create a more stable business environment, and have higher valuations. And, of the current US companies that export, 98% are small and midsized companies.[6]

Omer shares his experience starting and expanding an Israeli company and offers suggestions on how to think globally from the start.

GLOBAL IN ISRAEL—FROM THE START

Israeli startups are known worldwide for their research and development in highly technical areas such as life sciences, medical devices, biotech, and technology, yet they need funding to launch these companies into commercial markets. Microsoft and Oracle, for instance, run programs in Israel to catch these startups early and then transition them into their internal programs, grooming them until they are ready to penetrate bigger markets.

Israeli company leaders understand the importance of connecting with other Israeli leaders for introductions to larger, global companies for commercialization and funding, and to support each other while globally expanding their understanding of market differences, business environments, and

---

cultural variances. Israeli companies pre-build an international expansion strategy and budget. Omer walks us through three challenges he faced and provides suggestions for moving through them:

CHALLENGE # 1: UNDERSTAND YOUR TARGET MARKET

The most common mistake when trying to market internationally is to assume that prospects in the target country will behave exactly as those in the home country. They do not. Audiences differ from one country to another.

In moving his business from Israel to New York during the Covid pandemic, Omer learned this lesson firsthand. "The US is more 'polite' in terms of how sales calls are conducted," he explains. "They will listen and act like they are really interested, and then ignore your calls. It was baffling! Israelis are much more direct. They will tell you immediately if they are not interested." Cultural norms differ and it is critical to understand the rules of the game wherever you are trying to do business. "It had to happen a few more times before I understood that the feedback you got face to face in those meetings didn't mean a lot," adds Omer. Experiences like these demonstrate the steep learning curve you face when entering a new cultural market.

To increase your understanding, step outside of your own expectations. Be flexible and open-minded, and your efforts will more likely succeed. Omer gradually learned to understand the US cultural differences by being curious and consistent, and that led to his success in acquiring clients interested in working with his company.

CHALLENGE #2: KNOW THAT LOCAL BEHAVIORS IMPACT MARKETING COSTS

Marketing and advertising costs differ across countries. For example, marketers in the US and Western Europe pay high costs for Christmas advertising, whereas in Israel advertising costs do not skyrocket during the Christmas shopping season since fewer people celebrate Christmas there. Or parents in Belgium, for instance, behave differently than those in Belarus. When creating ads for baby formula in these countries, marketers must understand how families in each environment wean their babies from liquid to real food, or how they feel about formula versus breast milk.

Understanding how various holidays, behaviors, and priorities impact the local culture affects everything, from creative development to how to spend advertising dollars. Research your market before building a marketing budget and performance indicators.

CHALLENGE #3: FIND TRUSTED LOCALS

In your own country, you "get" the expectations and norms, plus you know who to turn to when you have questions about laws, taxes, financial systems, and how to get things done. A crucial challenge that arises when exporting goods to other countries is when you do not understand the inner workings of the system. As soon as possible, find trusted local business advisors in the new country – through your connections, embassies, consulates, and other business owners from your own country. There will always be cultural nuances and some chaos in the differences, yet with a trusted friend or advisor you can gain insights on how to grow, both personally and professionally.

SUPPORT FOR COMPANIES GOING INTERNATIONAL

Since most US companies do not think global from the start as those in Israel do, the federal and state governments offer free consulting assistance and grants to help those companies that want to export their goods and services. The balance of trade in the US, with more imports coming in than exports going out, means that we purchase more than we sell, notes Omer. He acknowledges that the US government offers these programs to help small and midsized companies export, since US companies are less experienced in global business and have a much higher learning curve. (Read more about these programs in the last couple of chapters of this book and find contact information in the Bonus Material.)

Omer's interview is a good reminder that accessing support from your network and spending time understanding the people, culture, and preferences of the local market highly increases an exporter's likelihood for success.

KEY POINTS TO REMEMBER:

- Think global from the start to set yourself up for current and future success.

- Take time to learn about cultural norms, preferences, and behaviors in each target market.

- Consult with trusted friends, colleagues, vendors, or government resources with familiarity in the new market for advice.

Hear Omer's full podcast episode at

- https://www.rapporttranslations.ccm/the-global-marketing-show/half-human-half-machine-for-global-growth

CHAPTER 2

DON'T GO TOO LITTLE, TOO SLOW

"In-person interactions are so important in building any kind of relationship."

—*Aytul Ercil, Vispera co-CEO*

Now that you're thinking global from the start, what might that look like? In this chapter we meet a CEO who has had success thinking big.

Selling a product or service internationally can be daunting and overwhelming. Yet, occasionally, we find a CEO who fearlessly goes international from the start. Why are some ready from the get-go and others wary of entering the international arena?

For many, readiness may simply be a by-product of circumstance and chance, according to Aytul Ercil, PhD, and guest on the *Global Marketing Show* (Episode 109). Aytul is an applied researcher and a co-founder and co-CEO of Vispera,[7] an image-recognition company that helps retailers gather information from the selling floor to track stocking, compliance, pricing, industrial planning, and design.

From the outset, Türkiye-based Vispera operated as a global company. "We were born global from the very first day, so we were never afraid of going international," says Aytul. "Because sales cycles are usually longer in

Türkiye than elsewhere, the Turkish population didn't trust us as much, so we looked outside of the country for our first clients. And I had lived in the US for nine years, so I understood international life."

Initially, clients found Vispera by word of mouth. The company built its website solely in English and yet, from inception, fielded requests from potential customers worldwide. In fact, the first sales request came from outside Türkiye. Afterward, Vispera quickly expanded into 11 countries, due simply to project extensions from that initial organization. Today, Vispera's technology is implemented in 62 countries, with clients such as Coca-Cola, Circle K, and Unilever.

Vispera survived their first four years without a dedicated salesperson or a marketing budget, growing organically through direct outreach and word of mouth. It was difficult – the company built slowly in South America and then entered North America, targeted to be its largest market. By responding to market demand and growing organically, the company has been able to hire experienced, in-country managing directors and open offices in Amsterdam (2020), Chicago (2021), and London (2022). The organization expects to grow by over 40% in the coming years and most of that will be outside its home country.

COMMON OBSTACLES TO INTERNATIONAL GROWTH

Vispera's focus on international growth is unusual for most startups, yet Aytul knew that by gaining a first-mover advantage and servicing recognized brands as clients, she positioned her company for greater success. Aytul cites the major challenges for startups seeking international sales as:

1. **Lack of Money to Hire Salespeople from the Start.** Initially, Aytul had to do ALL the outreach. Finding and hiring good salespeople took time. She explains, "You first need to build up your reputation in order to attract a good salesforce." She tried hiring a less expensive salesforce, but they "made mistakes because we couldn't afford good people. But over time, as we grew, we were able to hire better people."

She also learned that hiring salespeople in the target geographic markets provided the local physical presence needed to develop relationships to sell her technologies. "In-person interactions are so important in building any kind of relationship," she emphasizes. "And relationships lead to sales."

2. **Lack of Marketing Resources.** Instead of having an internal or outsourced team to develop a strategy, differentiation, and messaging, Aytul had to research the markets and develop the marketing materials completely on her own. That took significant time and effort.

3. **Limited Global Entrepreneurial Support.** Lack of connections to global business communities and venture capital "angels" makes international growth difficult for any startup. Aytul has a PhD in mathematics from Brown University; she's a very smart woman. Yet, she lacked business experience. "When I started my first company, we worked from project to project initially, instead of by building a product. That turned out to be a mistake," recalls Aytul. "But we had no alternative. We had no money, so we had to work that way." After many initial mistakes, especially in the financial arena, she learned through trial and error: "I didn't even know what a P&L [profit and loss] statement was at first! So, some of the financial decisions I made at first weren't good, but I learned." She acknowledges that if she had access to an international entrepreneurial community earlier, she would have had critical business information and support to allow her to make better decisions sooner.

OVERCOMING OBSTACLES

Having overcome these challenges, here are some of Aytul's suggestions to make your journey easier:

1. **Collaboration** – Prior to founding Vispera, Aytul started a company that provided imaging-based automatic inspection and analysis but experienced difficulties in selling simply because, at the time, no

one expected high-tech products from Türkiye. She had to think creatively about how to become recognized for her leading-edge technology. At a European Machine Vision Association (EMVA) conference, Aytul connected with a German company interested in partnering. Her company's trajectory improved dramatically once they began collaborating with the German company for two reasons: First, being from Germany, they had global recognition for high quality technology. Second, the German partners showed Aytul the advantages of working to create a product, rather than jumping from one project to another. "I think the key for any startup is to think creatively about your fundraising," advises Aytul. "[And] if you can find a partner to help, even better." Eventually the German company purchased her company, enabling Aytul and her R&D manager to benefit from the lessons they learned and launch Vispera.

2. **Leadership** – Aytul learned that having good local leadership is critical for growth. It starts with hiring solid leaders in each country that know the region, understand the industry, and have good management capabilities to create a strong team. They also increase sales faster by developing a pipeline of prospects through their connections.

3. **On-boarding Strategy** – As they grew, Aytul found that documenting the processes for new clients and new employees made their training and new market launches significantly easier.

4. **Alignment** – It is critical for everyone to be aligned around the same goals and vision (as we'll discuss in Chapter 12). If not, the entire sales effort and production process simply won't work. Everyone needs to agree on goals, sales, and deliverables.

5. **Consistent Communication** – Working across time zones, cultures, and product development is difficult and Aytul recognizes the challenges of keeping people connected. Her company conducts weekly meetings with in-country managing directors and monthly meetings with regional managers to discuss common goals and plans. The

company also conducts an annual three-day strategy meeting with global managers on go-to-market strategies, ensuring that marketing messages are consistent and globalized. "Basically, our clients have the same issues wherever they are. In some countries, like India, the problems may differ slightly since [their] stores are smaller mom-and-pops, but with large retailers the issues, criteria, and methods are pretty similar."

6. **English** – Even though the company is Turkish, the company language is English for a few reasons: the largest target market is the US, Aytul speaks fluent English, the company's technical vocabulary is relatively limited, and Vispera hires programmers who speak enough English to communicate with others.

7. **Flexibility** – Even though Aytul's company currently works in English, they built their software so that it can easily be customized into any language. This flexibility ensures that they can sell to global markets and service multinational companies.

8. **Translation** – When clients desire in-language support, her company hires bilingual employees and localizes or translates client materials.

9. **Perseverance and Resilience** – Resiliency is so important, especially when beginning an international venture. Things may not go your way initially, so the ability to pivot, refocus, and be flexible is a critical attribute to growing a company. Aytul says her mantra is to have "sabir"! (Patience!)

We find that there are two types of founders that think globally from the start – those that live in smaller countries with a limited market or those that have lived internationally and understand the potential of global markets.

Aytul is representative of both types – as a founder based in Türkiye she understood that for her product to succeed, she needed to go global from the start in order to meet the needs of her target clients: multinational companies. With her thoughtful approach to understanding her potential clients and her experience working internationally, she was motivated to think big from the start.

If you don't fall into either category, do NOT be discouraged. Take off your blinders, think creatively, and keep reading to hear more stories from those who have been there – like Brittany Cooper Kingdon in the next chapter who shares her cautionary tale about going too big, too quickly.

KEY POINTS TO REMEMBER:

- Learn, ask, and plan for the right sized launch.
- Keep asking your team members and customers about what works or needs to change.
- Be persistent and resilient in the face of challenges.

Hear Aytul's full podcast episode at

- https://www.rapporttranslations.com/the-global-marketing-show/applied-research-creates-tech-solutions

CHAPTER 3

DON'T GO TOO BIG, TOO FAST

"We had this passion for travel…but we were really naive about what it would take to be successful and get [the business] off the ground internationally."

—Brittany Cooper Kingdon, TourMe, Marketing Expert

Now that you've read about going global from the start and starting big, let's look at the flip side of that and build guardrails around going too fast. This next lesson parallels the story of *Goldilocks and the Three Bears* – don't go for the biggest, hottest bowl of porridge first or you may burn yourself. The same is true when embarking on a global marketing effort: It may be dangerous to jump into the global marketplace all at once, expanding too quickly or too broadly. Rather, do your research, plan strategically, and act thoughtfully, as Aytul Ercil did in Chapter 2. You will have much greater long-term success.

Brittany Cooper Kingdon, interviewed on the *Global Marketing Show* (Episode 14), began her career as the Marketing Automation Specialist at TourMe, a now defunct international tour and travel company that developed an app to connect tour guides and tourists. Reflecting on her first-hand experience about what to avoid during a global launch, she recalls that her experience at the international startup was negatively impacted by her lack of either marketing experience or appreciation for the importance of a marketing strategy and plan. She and her equally naive colleagues began their jobs eagerly: "We created messaging and ads to be distributed around the world, and quickly learned that there are rules...we had no idea that we would encounter cultural differences in the markets."

Clearly unprepared for what they faced, they soon learned that they were in over their heads. Yet by doing everything simultaneously, they also received immediate feedback about their mistakes, allowing them to adjust quickly. After spending a few weeks experimenting with various messages on social media, they learned a lot!

For instance, the team discovered that although they had a great idea, the marketing was all wrong. Tour guides and users were enthusiastic about the concept, and the two years spent developing the app resulted in a beautiful product. Yet they included the marketing research and legal teams much too late in the process to produce a successful launch—they thought global from the start but were not strategic in their execution. As Brittany explains, "We were running ads as soon as the app went live—we had so little experience in international marketing! [Official] tour guides were up in arms on Facebook and Instagram. We didn't realize that there were required licenses and background checks for tour companies and guides. Without any legal counsel then, we had no idea what we were doing." As a result, the company had to pull ads out of Asia, Africa, and other parts of the world. They realized that they had approached the launch completely wrong.

INCLUDE MARKETING EARLY AND HAVE A STRATEGIC PLAN

Because they had funding and tremendous excitement around the app, the group lost sight of its overall strategy and the precision required to get there. They needed to slow down and create a plan for the marketing launch. Looking back at the startup's experience, Brittany describes a host of approaches that, in retrospect, seem ill-planned and inappropriate: "We had this passion for travel and all these ideas, but we were really naive about what it would take to be successful and get it off the ground internationally."

She now knows that successful marketing takes strategy and forethought. Brittany suggests following these steps:

1. **Do Your Homework** – Without preparation, the team ran scattered rather than knowledgeably. Later in Chapter 4, Stephanie Hendricks describes how her company researched markets before acting. This chapter will provide good advice on how to do your homework before a product launch.

2. **Be Strategic** – Do not jump into using marketing tactics without a clear strategy behind them. This is a common error that so many young companies or startups make. In Brittany's situation, the startup relied on "organic" adoption rather than creating a strategic marketing plan to drive that adoption. Because they already developed their app, they believed that people would naturally find it. Instead, they needed to create more buzz in the marketplace for tourists rather than just focus on finding the tour guides. Without incoming customers to use the app, tour guides found the app useless.

3. **Start Small, Then Scale Up** – Pick a smart market, one you know or that makes sense from your research, to use as a testing ground. Consider how you generate revenue and create a process. Once you figure that out, you can replicate it. Brittany reflected that if TourMe had done this first, they would have been much more successful.

4. **Use a Measured Approach** – After your test market proves successful, continue to build it before starting a second market. Better to establish yourself in a few markets rather than be stretched thin in too many places.

5. **Follow the Cultural Norms** – Brittany admitted that TourMe's approach needed to be much more sensitive to the local languages and culture. While the startup's app included 25-30 languages, the marketing did not: "We were trying to do it cheaply and go big. But if we had narrowed it down, been more focused and strategic, we would have been more successful. We already had the app trans-

lated, so we felt pressure to go big!" As they began to launch ads, they relied solely on English rather than translating and adapting the messages. As a result, they lost out on a significant number of potential markets. Yet, once they translated their ads, they received great response. In Finland, because TourMe translated their marketing, they experienced tremendous success.

6. **Remember Your Audience** – Sometimes your target audience's language may not be the local language. When Brittany's company launched in Madrid, "We had to consider that tourists could be speaking various languages, not just Spanish. We needed to determine how to market to all the tourists across various languages." By remembering your buyers and delivering exactly what they want, you increase adoption…and your success.

Brittany's insights are hugely valuable to early-stage companies, which is why we chose to include her story. We appreciate her honesty, openness, and reflection on her time at TourMe. Since her role there, Brittany has succeeded in marketing roles at several other organizations. Her experiences serve as a good reminder that we all learn from mistakes. Building upon those insights and challenges creates success.

As Brittany recalls, although TourMe made many mistakes by trying to go too big, too fast, "One thing we did well was understanding how to communicate with others, being open-minded, and appreciating cultural differences. Although we had no revenue coming in, our outreach was effective."

TourMe did approach some aspects of launching a business correctly, especially thinking early about the global markets and translation. Too often, technology companies build their platforms without considering how to adapt for translation. Then these primarily English-speaking organizations plan international expansions into countries that speak only English regardless of competition, regulatory, laws, or low market demand. They suffer when non-English speaking clients request their products. There is certainly a sweet spot that you can identify to avoid the "hottest bowl" of trying to grow too quickly or the "cold bowl" of not thinking big enough. With a little preparation and strategy, you can find the "just right bowl" of expansion.

KEY POINTS TO REMEMBER:

- Plan ahead for a successful global launch.

- Start smaller and scale up as you enjoy successes.

- Cater your product and marketing to your target customer's language and cultural preferences for better results.

Hear Brittany's full podcast episode at

- https://www.rapporttranslations.com/the-global-marketing-show/startup-goes-global

CHAPTER 4

BE STRATEGIC

"The exercise itself of reflecting and considering can be very valuable."

—*Stephanie Hendricks, Voltus, Senior VP Operations and Customer Success*

I n Chapter 3 we learned some of the pitfalls that TourMe faced by launching internationally without proper preparation and strategy. Here, we will explore how researching and building a strategy first can lead to success.

As a former naval intelligence officer, Stephanie Hendricks' experience as a counter-terrorism analyst in Bahrain gave her a unique opportunity to develop skills in research and observation that conveniently converted into strategic business planning. Although she no longer needs to be as detailed as an intelligence officer, Stephanie's background benefits her in her position as Senior Vice President Operations and Customer Success at Voltus,[8] a demand response energy company.

In the *Global Marketing Show* (Episode 9), Stephanie explains why preparation and research are key to the planning process. By reflecting on your organization's current model, you can determine how to leverage your current capabilities. "The exercise itself of reflecting and considering can be very valuable," she notes. "It will show you how to use your current abilities and potentially open up new ones."

OPPORTUNITY FIRST, LANGUAGE SECOND

Naturally, deciding where to expand geographically takes thought, and the right decision will differ for each organization depending on its products or services, potential growth opportunities, connections, and language abilities. So how should you go about deciding? Stephanie emphasizes the importance of considering your company's growth and opportunities first and language issues second. When Voltus first looked at expanding beyond the US and Canada, the company researched several countries with a strong market for their products, starting with Mexico, Japan, Poland, and Australia. Ultimately, they chose Australia because the CEO previously worked there, understood the local market, and recognized the huge scalable growth opportunity.

The fact that Australians speak English was a bonus – no one had to learn a new language or hire an interpreter. Voltus still hired a local team in Australia to run operations smoothly in real time. Had they chosen Japan, language would have added an additional challenge. For Voltus, though, size and growth opportunity drove the location decision, not language.

"In our case, choosing Australia was a blend of the alternatives," notes Stephanie. "We knew we could find local partners on the ground who could use our name and leverage our go-to-market team. We could start small and leverage our assets. Language still played a role in our decision. We needed to consider language issues in our rollout, such as: Do we need an alternative website? What are the local rules? What form of English do we need to use? And what kind of technical hardware do they use?" Adapting US to Australian English was still important to make sure they connected with the local market.

Many organizations seem to fear handling local and regional culture when considering an international expansion. Yet, language and culture are not the best criteria for selecting a new market if the competition is higher or demand is lower in an English-speaking target market. It is best to consider the actual growth opportunities.

GO-TO-MARKET QUESTIONS

Stephanie also explained that once Voltus identified the next market for expansion, they had additional questions to answer, such as:

- Will we be the company of record or hire an intermediary for hiring local employees?
- For local representation, will we hire, acquire, or partner with locals to help with your rollout, even though they may not be as experienced in the overall business?
- What are the hardware and connectivity requirements?
- How will we handle shipping and logistics requirements?

At Voltus, the company leaders did not run from the challenge. In fact, they embraced it. "In our case, because we build our own hardware in Texas, we had to determine how much it would cost to ship to Australia. And, depending on the [electrical] outlets there, would we need new equipment? What was the Wi-Fi/cellular situation? All of these seemingly silly questions became very important," says Stephanie.

CREATIVE PROBLEM SOLVING

For strategy development, it is important to brainstorm what could affect the rollout and discuss how to handle these factors *before* starting. By anticipating as much as possible, the team becomes better equipped to handle unexpected challenges that arise.

"Location, or being remote, does not matter as much to our company," notes Stephanie. "It's all about creative problem solving. If you have a great team of translators, you only need to speak one language." And, by being creative, you don't need to eliminate employee talent because of language limitations. Finding ways to recruit, train, engage, and include employees across multiple languages makes the team healthier and more innovative. She reiterates that being inclusive across languages brings fresh ideas and creative solutions.

Creative problem solving also comes into play with lead generation and sales. Consider your company's sales strategy, prospecting methods, and marketing communications and whether they will be effective in the new country. Make sure that your strategy translates to the new environment, your outreach is culturally appropriate, and that your marketing materials and terms translate correctly. If you anticipate issues, research ways to adapt to the new environment. A professional translator or interpreter can help smooth the transition by culturally adapting your process and materials to be successful. Rather than measuring the cost of these services, think of the return on your investment when you clearly communicate and develop trust with prospects and clients.

As a leadership team evaluates whether and how to go global, strategic reflections and discussions about current business models often provide insights on how to improve domestic business or uncover creative ideas for expansion. Before jumping into a new market, it is worth taking the time to do the research and assess your differences and opportunities.

KEY POINTS TO REMEMBER:

- Choose a target market based on the opportunity for sales first, not differences in language and culture.

- Brainstorm potential issues and develop strategies for overcoming them before they arise.

- Increase opportunities by adapting your marketing messages and your employment practices to the new culture and language.

Hear Stephanie's full podcast episode at

- https://www.rapporttranslations.com/the-global-marketing-show/building-strategy-for-global-expansion

CHAPTER 5

RESEARCH DRIVES STRATEGY AND MITIGATES RISK

"Pick up local words and build bridges to people."

—John Jove, US Consumer Products Company, Vice President of Sales

To build a successful global strategy you need information and insight into your target market's preferences – what works there and what does not. This is where focused research comes into play.

On the *Global Marketing Show* (Episode 60), John Jove, Vice President at a global consumer products company, chuckles as he admits that when market research fails, funny stories and memes often result. These situations can be amusing, but they often result in poor sales or worse, damaged reputations. Conducting proper research and consulting experts can help avoid these issues.

John tells a story he heard about a US food company that tried to export snacks from the US to Mexico without developing a comprehensive launch strategy or conducting sufficient market research. Consumers in Mexico generally like US food products, but they were not familiar with this type of food. They found the type of snack confusing as they did not fully understand when and how to eat the product. Furthermore, the company later discovered significant Mexican food labeling regulations, which obliged them to pay for translated ingredient labels to be added manually.

Only after failing did the company realize their mistakes and acknowledge that they needed to do a better job at the marketing basics:

- Building awareness by educating the consumer and promoting the product through social media and digital marketing
- Engaging the consumer with sampling
- Encouraging purchase with in-store promotions

Simply because a product is popular in its home country does not mean it will do well elsewhere. This story emphasizes that successful global marketing efforts depend on doing the upfront research to understand local preferences and government regulations, then trying to address those needs as best as possible.

STARTING A RESEARCH EFFORT

The more informational interviews you conduct before arriving at a solution, the better you will understand your consumer's needs and desires. The first step in any research effort is to develop a hypothesis and approach responses qualitatively. Validate those hypotheses through quantitative testing. Once you begin to gather results, analysis becomes a bit of art and science. Start asking questions and analyze the data. "If you can get to an actionable point and take the insight that you developed and work it through your business processes to come up with a solution to a problem, or an opportunity for a consumer, then you will be successful," explains John.

THE **WHY** QUESTIONS

Think of your research as answering the *who, what, where, when, how,* and *why* questions before reaching conclusions on your go-to-market strategy.

Then dive into more *why* questions to get deeper insights. The following are examples of clarifying *why* questions market researchers can ask to increase their chances of a successful launch:

- **Why** did a consumer buy a certain product?
- **Why** did they select the size?
- **Why** was it right for them?
- **Why** was it right for that time of day?
- **Why** did they consider it?
- **Why** might they like the packaging?
- **Why** was it right for their occasion?

Once you ask the initial questions, see where they lead and ask more. The secret is to ask the right *why* questions, listen deeply, and take good notes. Then switch it up – ask *why* not questions, like "*why* didn't the consumer buy a product?" or "*why* didn't they select a size?" Asking both ways uncovers valuable information.

Afterward, John recommends that the research team shares the results internally across different organizational functions to improve their understanding of the consumer and their behavior. Ultimately, they look for trends and deeper meaning behind the answers.

PRELIMINARY RESEARCH

Naturally, extensive research is much easier for large multinational companies to conduct (i.e., Nestle, Nike, Procter & Gamble, Coca-Cola), since they have enormous operations, internal teams, and outside agencies to help them decipher consumer trends and insights. Smaller companies still need to do their research. Several tools and techniques that are helpful even without enormous budgets or internal research departments include:

- Searching for keywords in your online categories to look for patterns

- Examining Google analytics for search volumes
- Reviewing top trends in a category before launching a new product (particularly clothing, music, food)
- Visiting the country in person to observe buying behavior
- Finding local partners for advice
- Holding focus groups in person or online

By paying attention to trends, companies might uncover ideas for product launches. For example, busy new restaurant openings might signal local preferences for certain ethnic foods. Or a growing population of an ethnic group in a community could signal a higher demand for specific snacks. For example, the large population of Indians in eastern Canada purchases more Indian snacks than in western Canada where the larger East Asian communities prefer snacks with East Asian flavors.

As John points out, there are a wide variety of tools and ways to gather market intelligence that can help in the market research process.

MULTILINGUAL FOCUS GROUPS

Conducting focus groups in international target markets requires that language barriers be handled correctly to ensure accurate research results. John suggests that when organizations conduct multilingual focus groups, they have professionally translated materials and hire language service providers to handle cross-language communication. He says it is important to use human interpreters rather than automated translation to capture the contextual flavor often lost when relying on online or automatic translation tools. John also reminds us that just because populations share a language, they do not necessarily share a culture. For example, Brazilian Portuguese does not match the language spoken in Portugal, and even within a country local expressions and preferred slang or terminology can differ regionally – think soda vs. pop in the US. (We dive deeper into language and culture in later chapters.)

Each country or region bases local expressions on its specific history and culture. Over time, many languages merged where large immigrant influxes influenced the language and culture. In Brazil, for instance, Sao Paulo exhibits an Italian influence; Southern Brazil has a German influence; and near Argentina there is a mixture of Spanish and Portuguese. It is truly a smorgasbord of wonderfully mixed cultures and languages!

The best advice, John says, is to prepare by researching current issues, studying the language, and reading about the history: "Pick up local words and build bridges to people."

The point is – do your research. Today, the ease of access to the internet makes it so much faster and easier to understand what people value by looking at the culture, history, or geography online. In short, be creative about how you conduct your research.

OPPORTUNITY OR RISK

John considers the challenge of conducting international research as a mixture of expanding opportunity and limiting risk. Here are some additional inexpensive research tricks:

- Listen to podcasts from locals to hear actual opinions.
- Read local newspapers to stay current on news.
- Interview locals, colleagues, and contacts about current issues and preferences.
- Visit the country to watch people interact.
- Meet with potential partners and prospects.
- Use your senses – listen to local sounds, look at sites and colors, taste local foods, experience new smells, and feel the vibe.

Another simple yet effective way to learn about the culture is to listen to how people speak English as a second language. By mirroring styles in communication, you develop insights into how people in a culture think and act. Pay attention to word choices, hand movements, head nods, and body language. "Be careful, because in some cultures nodding the head means 'no, I don't agree,' and in others shaking the head means 'yes, I agree.' Be careful how you interpret the signals. Language and mannerisms are a way of adapting. Stay intentionally curious — hyperactively so!," John emphasizes.

INTENTIONAL CURIOSITY BUILDING RELATIONSHIPS

It takes time to develop a basic understanding of your target market. Without understanding your customer completely, your efforts can fail. John describes an experience he had in Brazil while tackling some business transformations and considering new ways of going to market: "I was thinking about the business processes, how we could be more efficient, but I hadn't built up significant rapport with my direct employees. My boss pulled me aside and said, 'You know, it's not so much how *much* you know, it's how much you *care*.' After I focused on the people, we gradually found ways to introduce the efficiencies in a go-to-market model that incorporated their local thinking. That lesson has stuck with me ever since." Establishing caring, genuine relationships with employees and business partners will get you farther than solely focusing on efficient business processes.

We touched upon language and culture several times throughout these stories about laying the groundwork for an international launch. In the next section we will take a deeper dive into these considerations.

KEY POINTS TO REMEMBER:

- Do your research first to avoid becoming an amusing tale.
- Look beyond the internet and use more interactive research methods for a deeper understanding.
- Confirm your research findings to limit your risk.

Hear John's full podcast episode at

- https://www.rapporttranslations.com/the-global-marketing-show/five-tricks-language-and-culture

NAVIGATING LANGUAGE AND CULTURE

CHAPTER 6

CONSOLIDATE YOUR GLOBAL MESSAGE

"Since adding translation, our website sessions have increased by 85% in Spanish-speaking countries, 158% in Indonesia, and 22% in China."

—*Michelle Safrit, Conitex Sonoco, Marketing Manager*

You may think that a good way to handle language and culture differences is to have each location manage the local marketing. This is not ideal when you are trying to build a cohesive global brand and reputation. Here's a story about one company's challenges and solutions for dealing with this type of disjointed marketing plan.

"I started to look at our website and realized there were several different website versions, and then started uncovering more and more websites all over the world…Greece, China, Taiwan…" confesses Michelle Safrit, Marketing Manager at Conitex Sonoco,[9] a manufacturer and provider of packaging/shipping materials. As Michelle delved deeper, she uncovered over 50 new products with varying messages for new markets – a global marketer's nightmare! On the *Global Marketing Show* (Episode 8), Michelle retells her story.

Through acquisitions and fast decentralized growth, Conitex Sonoco's brand became fragmented, product descriptions were unclear, and inefficient marketing led to wasted time and money. With support from senior management, Michelle clarified the actions needed for creating a global marketing effort, by:

- Identifying all current global sites
- Developing an outline of product offerings by country
- Establishing global brand guidelines
- Clarifying differentiation and messaging
- Adapting the messaging for each market
- Localizing product offerings by market
- Translating appropriate content

Michelle learned the following lessons during the process at Conitex Sonoco:

UNDERSTAND YOUR NEEDS

First, Michelle asked several key division leaders to share their product availability by location so she could clearly identify the product offerings and translation requirements. At first, Conitex Sonoco thought they would use a machine translation service with post-human editing. But, after reviewing a few pages, they realized the quality was extremely poor. They changed course as they realized they needed professional translators who could understand the local culture and provide high-quality marketing translation. In addition to quality issues, the machine translation approach did not work with their HubSpot-built website because each page layout was unique. They needed real people who could pay attention to the context of the information and build the site correctly.

CONSIDER YOUR RESOURCES

When Michelle reached out to their marketing agency for advice, they recommended partnering with specialists in marketing translation who could bring them high quality results. Working in partnership with the marketing agency, Rapport International provided professional translation ready to be manually uploaded to display correctly on the website – including clear navigation for each country and language. Michelle reflected on working with the team, "We didn't have to worry, and that speaks to the value of having a partner in translation services [work with our creative agency]."

Note: *If you are considering using machine or AI translation tools like Google Translate or ChatGPT, continue reading, as we will discuss the history and appropriate uses for these technologies in the next chapter.*

TRANSLATE WITH THE LOCAL MARKET

Michelle understood that not everyone speaks the same language or communicates in the same way – even if they do share a language. To attain the best quality translation for marketing, she knew she needed professional translations that were culturally adapted to address regional colloquialisms. Sometimes words in one language or culture convey different meanings in another, and she wanted to make sure that they presented the company appropriately in all locations. For example, she found that marketers in Taiwan use stronger self-promotion words than in the US. By having local, native-language-speaking employees review the professional translations, she enhanced local communications while retaining the strength of their global brand.

Their optimal process had Rapport International doing the translation and coordinating with a local employee to review and track suggested changes. Then, the professional translator reviewed the edits and accepted changes that made sense and retained correct grammar. This process retained the global brand messaging while allowing for local adaptation.

GUIDE REGIONAL INTERNAL REVIEWERS CAREFULLY

Conitex Sonoco's bilingual general managers reviewed the website translations only after Michelle guided them on how to review the content so that the translations maintained the "globalized" marketing message instead of creating separate country messaging.

A "globalized" translation is understandable to anyone who speaks that language, no matter the country or region. Whereas a "localized" translation is specific to a local area, as it captures the area's colloquialisms, culture, idiosyncrasies, and visuals.

Initially, the Spanish manager had issues with the translations for his region. But once he understood that they "globalized" the Spanish for worldwide marketing, he reviewed and accepted the translations with only minimal suggestions. He realized that a globally recognized brand could help his market grow faster. By consolidating the global messaging, Conitex Sonoco reduced costs and demonstrated its global reach, a huge advantage in their industry.

BUILD A GLOSSARY FOR CONSISTENCY

Michelle knew that whether they localized or globalized, they needed to keep industry- or company-specific terms consistent. She worked with Rapport International to build a glossary in each language for both the translators and the reviewers to use. This kept the language consistent, especially with technical terms that do not have direct translations. Agreeing on specific terminology and adding them to a glossary helped keep all their materials consistent.

By consolidating and globalizing their website and marketing, Conitex Sonoco strengthened their global brand. They quickly learned that scattered, decentralized marketing would not help them build a reputation and grow sales.

In the next chapter we'll dive deeper into one of the lessons they learned: AI or machine translation tools are not good enough when translation matters.

KEY POINTS TO REMEMBER:

- Centralize marketing efforts to maintain a consistent brand message across markets.

- Globalize your translations to reach all the speakers of a language located around the world or localize it to appeal to people in a specific location or region.

- Work with a professional language service provider that specializes in marketing translation to streamline your global marketing processes.

Hear Michelle's full podcast episode at

- https://www.rapporttranslations.com/the-global-marketing-show/handle-website-translation

CHAPTER 7

INSIDER'S PERSPECTIVE ON AI AND TRANSLATION

"Google Translate makes bad translation free."
—*Adam Bittlingmayer, ModelFront, CEO*

L et's repeat that quote! "Google Translate makes bad translation free," says Adam Bittlingmayer, who worked at Google Translate in its early years and is an industry expert on automated translation. He happily admits that Google Translate is not a reliable source for high-quality translation, as the team at Conitex Sonoco quickly discovered in the last chapter, but he points out that most people in the world can only access most content thanks to automatic translation.

Adam, guest on the *Global Marketing Show* (Episode 116), is now CEO and co-founder of ModelFront,[10] a company "making human-quality translation radically more efficient" by determining which machine-translated sentences can fully skip review and editing by humans.

HISTORY OF AUTOMATED TRANSLATION TOOLS

In order to understand whether automated translation will actually replace humans, we need to look at the history of automated translation and its current state. Technological initiatives to translate languages began back in the 1940s after wartime success in code breaking. Funding increased dramatically in machine translation research and by 1954, the first demonstration on machine translation impressed people enough to generate massive funding.

Built with bilingual dictionaries that provided word-for-word translation, people soon recognized these early systems as insufficient even when linguists contributed formal grammar rules to expand them. Researchers encountered "semantic barriers" that led to disappointing results. In 1966, a report from MIT concluded that "there is no immediate or predictable prospect of useful machine translation," yet it suggested developing tools for professional translators. After the report, funding slowed in the US but continued in other countries for different methodologies and uses – such as weather reporting, which uses limited and repetitive vocabulary. In the 1980s, the increase of mainframe computing systems and microcomputers contributed to the development of a wide variety of machine translation systems, yet none were good enough for general use.[11]

In the 1990s, four *major* developments happened:

- IBM researchers published results using statistical methods (replacing dictionaries).

- Japanese groups began using "example-based" translations.

- Global researchers started innovating in speech translation.

- Trados Studio released the first translation memory (TM) for professional translators.

These developments led the way for creative thinking through the 1990s when the industry saw fast growth for translation memories and translation aids used by professional translators to avoid having to translate the same materials over again. Large corporations found time and cost efficiencies for "good enough quality" where large amounts of content repeated each year – for example, car user manuals. Without translation memories and automation, human translation would be so terribly painful and inefficient that buyers would procure less translation, not more.

And did jobs disappear? No! Jobs in the language services industry grew by orders of magnitude. Language service providers still struggle to find highly qualified linguists.

Statistical machine translations progressed through the 2000s into neural machine and AI translation tools. We saw the launch of Google Translate in 2006 and the continual improvements in that platform. Although quality improved because of the i) larger availability of bilingual memories, ii) open-source availability of software, and iii) availability of quality evaluating metrics, challenges continued in all the automated systems that include:

1. Lack of cultural understanding needed to reorder sentences to make grammatical sense to the reader.

2. Inability to handle morphologically rich languages like Spanish or French that use conjugation to signify gender, formality, number, or tense.

3. Challenges with words that convey an unpredictable, precise meaning in the original language, or the way words are combined to make new meanings.

4. Difficulty in handling words with no direct translation or with multiple translations.

5. Problems with transliterating names (converting the letters or characters from one writing system to another while maintaining the meaning).

6. Issues with the treatment of pronouns.

Even with these issues, the simplified access to translation again elevated demand for translation, as content that would not have been translated got translated and people who would not have had access to translation received access.

People in the language services industry have been using automation tools for a long time, yet researchers still have not figured out how to provide quality equal to a human translator without a 100% match using a translation memory already reviewed by a professional for an earlier project. Yet, the advances in technology enable access to translation, create efficiencies for companies and linguists, and support globalization.

HAND WORKERS TO MOUTH WORKERS

Translators often call translation "the world's second oldest profession." It was one of the first that led humanity's transition from "hand workers" to a new breed known as "mouth workers." This intriguing and slightly humorous concept, in German slang, captures the essence of individuals who earn a living by talking and writing rather than by manual labor.

For example, "mouth workers" encompasses professionals like lawyers, startup CEOs, and marketers – those who rely on linguistic dexterity and verbal finesse to navigate their domains.

One of the big questions today is whether AI will most impact the "mouth workers" or the "hand workers." In earlier waves of automation, technology most impacted the "hand workers" by automating their jobs with tractors, dishwashers, and assembly lines. If we stretch this concept to encompass the change in the language services industry, we can say that translation always consisted of some "mouth work" – researching a product and its competitors to invent the Spanish term for a new feature, for example, but also a lot of very repetitive "hand work" – like changing an ASCII apostrophe to a curly apostrophe a million times.

The goal of automation, from translation memories to AI like ModelFront, aims to reduce the "hand work" so that the job becomes the value-added "mouth work."

POLARIZATION IN THE TRANSLATION INDUSTRY

Adam highlighted the current polarization in the translation industry, with translation teams facing pressure from both ends. Economic pressures and executive interest push the use of automation without understanding the intricacies of appropriate usage. Traditionalists, on the other hand, resist machine translation entirely because they understand the flaws. The challenge lies in finding appropriate uses for automation and designating materials for human involvement so that organizations can find a middle ground that balances quality, cost, and scalability.

WHO BENEFITS FROM AUTOMATED TRANSLATION?

For enterprise organizations that translate millions of words, automated translation solves a huge problem. Fashion marketplaces, online retailers, computer manufacturers, and online travel agencies all create tons of content – hundreds of millions of words – that are updated promptly and continually. Human translators cannot keep up with demand and the cost is astronomical. To handle these needs, forward-thinking organizations develop strict content guidelines and use machine translation (MT) with post-editing by a human (MTPE) to develop a translation memory system (TMS) to recall previously translated words or segments. This results in 50-90% of content being translated before a human must look at it for completeness, a huge time savings for translators.

Adam sees potential in the use of MT and AI translation for customer support, e-learning, and certain technical documentation – like automotive manuals that have constrained content and high volume (over 5 million words per year). Companies with high volume translation can build a LangOps (Language Operations) team that sets a strategic vision for multilingual communications, identifies content appropriate for automation, manages the technology, maintains glossaries and translation databases, and ensures an effective translation process. For consistency and accuracy, LangOps needs to work closely with marketing, sales, customer service, product management, communications, and content creation teams. Without high volume, it's just too hard for a LangOps team to justify the upfront setup or build the dataset required to make AI a worthwhile investment.

THE FUTURE OF TRANSLATION: A BALANCED COEXISTENCE

Contrary to the notion of automated content creation replacing human translation, Adam envisions a future where the two interact – because that's what he already sees happening. While tools like ChatGPT enhance efficiency, the need for high-quality, nuanced translations persists, ensuring a coexistence of machine and human contributions. In Adam's parting words, he encourages everyone to explore these language tools firsthand. Whether it's ChatGPT, DeepL, or Google Translate, the key is to play, experiment, and gain insights into their capabilities and limitations. As the language industry undergoes a transformation, understanding these tools empowers individuals to adapt and thrive in the evolving landscape.

In essence, the journey from "hand workers" to "mouth workers" symbolizes a broader shift in how we leverage language and technology – a journey that promises innovation, efficiency, and a harmonious coexistence of human and machine contributions.

A discussion about language cannot be complete without addressing culture. A country's culture influences language and behavior, so a marketing campaign that only addresses language differences is incomplete. Next, we will hear stories about adapting to and embracing local culture and customs to build relationships and trust.

KEY POINTS TO REMEMBER:

- Do not use automated translation tools when the content needs to be accurate and culturally adapted.

- Hire a professional language service provider that continues to evolve as technologies improve and change.

- Create a LangOps department to oversee the use of translation tools if you have a high volume of translation you want to automate.

Hear Adam's full podcast episode at

- https://www.rapporttranslations.com/the-global-marketing-show/ai-translation-inside-perspective

CHAPTER 8

CONQUER CULTURAL ISSUES

"Most people…look at culture through their own lenses."

—*Carole Copeland Thomas, C Thomas & Associates, Founder*

N avigating cultural differences while building a company culture or consistent brand voice can be challenging. Yet it is not insurmountable, especially with support from knowledgeable experts and a willingness to learn.

Suppose that the US team of an international organization blames "the Chinese" team for all the current mistakes and communication issues, and the Chinese team becomes frustrated when its US counterpart "behaves inappropriately." How should you address this situation?

Carole Copeland Thomas, founder of C Thomas & Associates,[12] joined as a guest on the *Global Marketing Show* (Episode 131) to discuss how to successfully navigate cultural issues such as these.

Culture is nebulous – we know what it is, yet it is difficult to define. As an expert in diversity, equity, and inclusion (DEI) for nearly 40 years, Carole describes culture as a concept that encompasses the social norms, behaviors, knowledge, arts, beliefs, customs, and habits of a group of people. She further explains it through the "Iceberg Model of Culture" that Edward T. Hall developed in 1976.

According to this model, the *top of the iceberg* stays visible to everyone: it contains a community's fine arts, literature, music, food, games, and dress. People outside of the culture clearly see these superficial elements. The *bottom of the iceberg*, the biggest part of a culture, hides beneath the surface. This includes aspects such as:

- **Eye Contact** – In the US, children learn the importance of direct eye contact. In Japan, children learn the opposite: that direct eye contact can be rude and considered aggressive and disrespectful.

- **Time** – Some cultures view time strictly and others allow flexibility. In Germany and Denmark, for instance, meetings start at the appointed time. Yet in other countries they are more fluid and laid back, running on, as Carole explains in her words, "CP time" (colored people time), "India time," or "island time".

- **Personal Space** – People have varying levels of comfort with touching, standing close together, and holding hands with friends. In North America, people typically prefer a distance of "arm's length," while Europeans accept "wrist length," and Middle Easterners welcome "elbow length" interactions.

- **Gestures** – In India, people may shake or "bobble" their head side-to-side to mean "I hear you" or "I don't know," or to say "yes" or "no." The closest conversational response in the US would be the equivalent of the expression, "Hmmm."

These examples show only a small number of the cultural components that could affect an organization's co-workers. Other aspects include:

- Approaches to problem solving

- Notions of leadership

- Tempo of work

- Patterns of group decision-making

- Status mobility

- Ideas about logic and validity

- Conversational patterns

While most people understand their own cultural norms, they do not realize how much cultural differences affect interpersonal relationships. Carole shares some of the misunderstandings she has helped navigate:

TRICKY SITUATIONS

A client had an employee from a Caribbean island where people in the workplace commonly touched one another, even members of the opposite sex. This behavior caused considerable issues because others misconstrued these actions as inappropriate. By understanding the cultural component and explaining expectations to everyone involved, Carole restored a respectful environment that reaffirmed more solid working relationships.

Another client hired a young manager to lead a team of about 25, including a dozen employees older than the manager. Unbeknownst to the manager, the older Black members of the team were more accustomed to being addressed as Mr. or Ms. out of respect for their age. Resentment grew within the team until Carole and the manager uncovered the issue and found appropriate ways for the manager to address the workers. In some cultures, age commands more respect, while in others, organizational position does. Navigating through these differences can be difficult yet not insurmountable.

Even as an expert in cultural issues, Carole admits that she sometimes runs into situations of her own. When she first became a grandmother, she wanted to choose a special name rather than being called "grandma" like her mother. Since she travels to Kenya frequently, she decided to adopt the Swahili name "Nyanya" for grandma. Her granddaughters called her Nyanya for years, but later Carole learned that the familiar name for grandma is actually "Bibi." Her granddaughters had been calling her the formal name for grandmother ("great mother"), or "tomato" – another translation of Nyanya!

SOLUTIONS

Whenever Carole enters a situation, her plan is to build rapport and alignment. First, she assesses the manager. If the manager is astute and wants to improve relationships, she knows that she will be able to work with them. Next, she teaches them to:

1. Develop rapport with each individual on the team. This does not mean prying into personal matters; it means getting to know everyone on an individual and professional basis. She recommends strategies such as scheduling time for coffee, lunch, or a conversation with no set agenda. Even if there are 40 people on the team, it is still worth the time to meet with each person.

2. Reflect upon the strengths and weaknesses of the team to understand what people contribute. Perhaps, she says, even doing a Strengths, Weaknesses, Opportunities, and Threats (SWOT) analysis on the personalities will yield a more accurate picture of the dynamics.

3. Communicate a vision to rally the team to work together toward shared goals. A shared vision, as we will discuss in Chapter 12, unites people as they focus on achievement together, depend on each other for diverse contributions, and celebrate as they reach milestones.

TROUBLE AREAS

Of course, these steps sound easy, but in practicality, difficulties arise. Carole explains the key areas that typically challenge leaders even after building relationships. These cultural elements may contribute to the continued dysfunction.

First, keep in mind that most people, including yourself, look at culture through their own lenses. Look at the US American culture as an example of how culture permeates local life. Many non-Americans consider Americans to be *perennial optimists.* This optimistic bend ties directly to US history: European immigrants came to the US looking for a better life, homesteaders moved west for land, and gold rushers believed they would find wealth in western states like California.

This pervasive US optimism affects American practices in many places. For example, if you ask, "How are you?" Americans reflexively answer, "Good." In giving feedback, Americans often couch negative feedback between positive statements. Just think of the "sh*t sandwich," where a person says something nice, gives negative feedback, then ends with a positive reflection. People from other cultures do not understand this practice – they leave confused as to whether they heard compliments or reprimands. In other cultures, negative feedback is much clearer and more direct.

Similarly, optimism in the American educational grading system treats perfect grades as attainable, while in many other countries, students' grades are based on ideals. In many places, receiving 15/20 on an assignment represents a project well done with room for improvement. In the US, though, students who get As or 5/5 have no room for improvement. Teachers, managers, and leaders benefit from clear explanations when giving cross-cultural evaluations or feedback to avoid confusion or hard feelings.

Second, keep doors open to knowing each other. Holding a single meeting to build rapport will not solve all issues. Continue the conversations to understand where opposite perspectives or points of view arise and contribute to issues.

Third, keep trying. High context languages such as Chinese or Japanese consider the context *around* the language and actions more important than the meaning of specific words. Low context languages, such as American and Canadian English and Dutch, are more literal. "Yes" means "yes" and "no" means "no." But in a high context culture, there may not necessarily be a true "no."

For example, when I (author Wendy MacKenzie Pease) lived in Taiwan as a child and a local friend asked if I wanted something to eat, I learned to say "no" multiple times to be polite. Yet I knew that eventually I would get treats anyway. Back in the US, I quickly learned that if I said "no" when offered treats, I missed an opportunity. This difference in responding is often referred to as the Yes-No Conundrum. Some languages, like Mandarin, may use the word yes but might have various levels of yes: the yes-yes, yes-maybe, and yes-no.

Fourth, prepare. Watching YouTube videos can teach you a lot about cultural subtext and non-verbal signals. What you wear for a meeting, where the meeting is held, or where people sit at the table holds great importance and sends different signals. Prior to entering a new business environment, experienced professionals research the differences between the home and new culture to understand the context of cultural communications and be better prepared.

HERE ARE SOME TRICKS TO WORKING CROSS-CULTURALLY:

1. **Ask open-ended questions.** Although it may seem better at first to ask simpler questions, you may get frustrated because of the yes-no conundrum or the Indian head bob. Rather than asking if the project will be finished by Friday, ask, "When will the project be completed?"

2. **Learn about your own culture.** Raise your awareness about your native culture. Often, we do not realize that the way we do things naturally – without thinking – can impact how we approach or react to certain situations. Culture is most invisible to its own participants. Try watching American comedians who make self-deprecating fun of "Americans!"

3. **Do a Gap Analysis.** Once you understand your culture, compare it to the other culture and notice the gaps. Knowing the gaps to navigate helps you succeed faster. In the next chapter, our guest introduces us to a framework for assessing those gaps.

4. **Read the room.** Successfully operating cross-culturally works better if you use all five of your senses to act and respond. Yes, it will challenge you more, but success is so wonderful.

5. **Keep trying.** Network with others to keep learning. Contact colleagues and ask for introductions at local embassies, companies, or organizations to get tips about cultural differences and how to navigate them. Interpreters are a great resource for facilitating conversations and serving as a cultural conduit to assist with communication beyond words in real-time.

6. **Ask for forgiveness**! Reach out, engage, and try. People forgive mistakes from visitors who are friendly and curious.

Remember our Chinese/English team struggling at the beginning of the chapter? Hopefully, now you have insights into how to step back and assess a situation and then step in to build a high-functioning team. Along with building rapport, many guests of the *Global Marketing Show* suggest that you "stay curious!" In the next chapter, we delve into that advice to understand more.

KEY POINTS TO REMEMBER:

- Build rapport!
- Understand your home culture's influences and accept the challenge to learn.
- Stay curious to grow and prosper.
- Forgive yourself and others for missteps.

Hear Carole's full podcast episode at

- https://www.rapporttranslations.com/the-global-marketing-show/rapport-across-cultures

CHAPTER 9

STAY CURIOUS AND MAKE CONNECTIONS

"People really just want the same things…when you boil it down, cultures are really so similar."

—Nick Canfield, Global Hola, co-Founder

S tay curious" was a key point in the last chapter and a mantra of many podcast guests. Let's dive deeper into understanding cultural styles and differences with Nick Canfield, co-founder of Global Hola,[13] a virtual assistant company for small business and guest on the *Global Marketing Show* (Episode 16).

Although English is often thought of as the global language, if you want to truly succeed when conducting "glocal" (local done global) business, you will need to embrace and use the local language. However, language includes more than words. Language captures a way of thinking and acting. As Nick says, "In short, yes, English is the global language, but if you want to be successful – no. To be successful in a lot of markets, you have to take an interest in, learn, and really appreciate the culture you are in. If you do not, you are not going to connect [with] or win clients." Perhaps if the employees in the Chinese/US company from the last chapter understood each other's cultures better, they could have avoided tension and formed positive relationships earlier. Let's consider ways to gain an understanding of people across cultures.

BE CURIOUS ABOUT CULTURE

Even before doing international business, Nick understood that culture affects success, so he studied how cultures vary by examining the late Dutch social psychologist, Geert Hofstede, and his work. Hofstede is well known for his "cultural dimensions theory" and "values survey model," which describes how cultures and their value systems can be broken into six categories:

- **Power Distance** – "This dimension deals with the fact that all individuals in societies are not equal – it expresses the attitude of the culture towards these inequalities amongst us."[14] As Nick explains, the US Constitution states that "all men are created equal," thus the nation strives for equality and the ability for all to speak up, while in other countries people accept that certain people (i.e., the boss) have more power and authority, therefore questioning them is unacceptable. Understanding the nuances of the local rules of hierarchy means that you act appropriately for the situation. For instance, in Costa Rica, using the informal pronoun for "you" in a formal situation can be a grave mistake. In Vietnam, using the correct pronouns for "you" expresses formality by noting differences in age or gender between speakers – using the wrong word may offend people.

- **Individualism** – "The fundamental issue addressed by this dimension is the degree of interdependence a society maintains among its members. It has to do with whether people's self-image is defined in terms of 'I' or 'we.'"[15] Americans, for instance, rank high on individualism and the self, which means not wanting to relinquish power to authorities. Nick observed that in Vietnam, Thailand, Japan, Korea, and Cambodia, on the other hand, collectivism and community are highly valued. People focus more on doing things for others and less on getting people to do things that would benefit only themselves. Entrepreneurship is easier to encourage in individualistic cultures.

- **Motivation to Achieve** – Cultures high in this category are driven by competition, achievement, and success with a clear winner or best in field. This value system starts in school and continues throughout life. A low score, on the other hand, shows a consensus-oriented society with value placed on caring for others and quality of life. Standing out from the crowd is not admirable. High and low motivation is separated by wanting to be the best versus liking what you do.

- **Uncertainty Avoidance** – We all have to deal with the unknown, yet people and cultures develop different ways to handle the anxiety that comes from ambiguity. Some try to control it while others believe in just letting it happen. Uncertainty avoidance is not risk-avoidance nor following the rules; it deals with the anxiety or distrust experienced when faced with the unknown. Some cultures prefer fixed habits and rituals and want to have expectations in the midst of the unknown, while others will wait it out to see what happens. Knowing this gives insight into negotiations or reactions.

- **Long-term Orientation** – Balancing links to the past while dealing with the challenges of the present and future varies across cultures. Low score cultures on this dimension prefer to maintain time-honored traditions and view societal change with suspicion. "Those with a culture which scores high, on the other hand, take a more pragmatic approach: they encourage thrift and efforts in modern education as a way to prepare for the future."[16]

- **Indulgence** – "One challenge that confronts humanity, now and in the past, is the degree to which small children are socialized. Without socialization we do not become 'human.' This dimension is defined as the extent to which people try to control their desires and impulses, based on the way they were raised. Relatively weak control is called 'Indulgence' and relatively strong control is called 'Restraint.' Cultures can, therefore, be described as Indulgent or Restrained."[17]

  - People in the US have high indulgent scores and high motivation for achievement – two dimensions we would not expect to see together. This certainly gives us insight into the common US saying "Work Hard, Play Hard."

Using the Hofstede Culture Model is a good way to understand the cultural differences between you and your international associates – look for areas where you differ to anticipate where conflict or misunderstanding may arise. By taking time to discuss these differences, you build trust and clarity.

OBSERVE BEHAVIORS

Along with the research, it helps to pay attention to behaviors. Nick explained that in the US, people jump into business discussions and negotiations without getting to know the other person. But through his travels in Asia, he learned that it is important to build relationships before conducting business. In Vietnam, for instance, having a beer with your business counterparts is a necessary first step before discussing anything substantial. "It's a big part of Asian business culture and bonding. They want to see how you are at your best…and at your drunkest!"

In Costa Rica, people need to warm up to you. Nick learned to avoid discussing business until the end of the conversation. "It's all about building relationships. Have coffee, relax, and be patient." In Micronesia, Nicks says, "It's all about kava. People socialize while drinking kava, a sedative-based drink. It's a big part of the culture. Kava bars are all over the place. If you drink kava with them, it shows you can be trusted, you're willing to help. You won't just be seen as the American with a brand-new project."

Learning about the local traditions and norms, as Nick points out, is the best way to connect to people on a deeper level and build relationships: "People really just want the same things…when you boil it down, cultures are really so similar. We all just want to have a family, be comfortable, have some meaning in life, eat some good food, and party sometimes!"

It is the small, local ways of relating to one another that translate into good relationship skills. And these are what can make or break a business relationship.

TRANSLATE INTO THE LOCAL LANGUAGE

Nick does emphasize that if you want to connect to people on the deepest level – for selling, business, or education – translating into the local language is the key to truly building an enduring relationship. "If your marketing messaging uses a culturally appropriate and local language approach, you will have a much better outcome." In his work in Micronesia, Nick learned that people often spoke English to communicate with residents of other islands. But for him to get attention on the islands, they had to translate materials into each island's specific language. Even though people spoke English, when making decisions or buying products they wanted native-language information that made cultural sense.

Nick's final suggestion for success: "Be friendly, open, vulnerable, and curious, wherever you are." By building relationships, you build trust. Speaking of trust, selling as a non-native takes a special set of skills. Let's move on to the next chapter to learn how Zach Selch does it.

KEY POINTS TO REMEMBER:

- Remember that English is NOT the global language even if many people seem to speak it well.

- Try, even if you fail, to communicate in the local language, as that goes a long way in building trust.

- Research and observe cultural differences to gain an understanding of expectations and potential offenses.

Hear Nick's full podcast episode at

- https://www.rapporttranslations.com/the-global-marketing-show/truly-global-millennial

CHAPTER 10

BUILD TRUST FOR INTERNATIONAL SALES

"No one in the world will make expensive purchases without trusting the other party."

—*Zach Selch, Global Sales Mentor, Principal*

Relationships formed on a foundation of cultural understanding are a great step toward building trust, an integral ingredient for success. How do you nurture and strengthen trust across culture and distance?

"My goal is to speak 150 words in as many languages as possible," comments Zach Selch, Principal at Global Sales Mentor[18] and guest on the *Global Marketing Show* (Episode 25). Yet when traveling for business, he uses his words primarily for speaking with taxi drivers, ordering at restaurants, and social interactions. He notes that, "It is so difficult to speak business in another language [that] I do not do it because of the risk of mistakes."

Zach is a specialist in international sales who previously served in the military, and he has an interesting take on sales and marketing. He describes the difference as: "sales is the infantry" and "marketing is the artillery" – you need both to be successful in growing international business. Instead of trying to do both, Zach focuses on direct sales by either representing a client company in international markets, building and training their local sales force, or finding a distributor to do the selling for the company. Through this work he has witnessed a vast variety of mistakes, including:

- **Entering the wrong market** – Without a deliberate strategy and the right connections, expansion efforts will fail when those involved do not see results quickly enough.

- **Hiring the wrong distributor** – Take the time to find a distributor that is the right size, has the relevant experience and connections, and demonstrates an aptitude and interest in showcasing your product as a primary, not forgotten one.

- **Using remote teams to sell** – Some companies think that they can sell from afar. You must have "boots on the ground" to stay in touch with the local market.

- **Not getting people together** – Although technology allows for remote meetings, companies that take the time and spend the money to get people together physically do better.

And, most important,

- **Not establishing trust** – People buy from people they trust. When dealing with higher value products and services, Zach insists on the importance of creating trust between the buyer and seller. No one in the world will make expensive purchases without trusting the other party.

BUILDING TRUST IN DIFFERENT CULTURES

Each culture creates trust in different ways. Zach explains that some cultures quickly trust while others take time and effort. Americans tend to trust quickly and may even spend $6,000 on an online purchase if they recognize the brand and URL. Whereas in Nigeria, trust is lower. Nigerians feel more comfortable working with a trusted salesperson from their network. When entering a new country, Zach makes sure to understand how people create trust so he can support buyers in the sales process.

Here are some of Zach's suggestions on how to build trust:

1. **Provide accurate translations!** If people cannot understand you, they will not buy. According to a CSA Research report titled "Can't Read, Won't Buy," 75% of buyers want reviews in their own language and 40% will not buy unless content is in their own language.[19]

2. **Make information accessible at the right time.** By providing easy access to sales sheets, marketing materials, and the buying process, prospects can research your products and services on their own time. For the final sales steps, accessible sales representatives can close the deal and dramatically increase sales.

3. **Provide local support to clients in creative ways.** At times, Zach will pay a local person to find and then hand their phone (with Zach on the line) to the high-level person he wants to talk to.

QUALITY TRANSLATION FUELS GROWTH & BUILDS TRUST

A cautionary note on translation – sometimes, Zach sees companies try to save money on translation by asking their distributors to translate for them. This can be a huge mistake because they serve as your hired sales force. Although distributors may know English well enough to speak with you, they typically do not have the correct grammar and writing skills to be professional translators. This can lead to problems, such as: inaccurate information being released in the market, lost productive selling time, "message creep" where your statements become inflated (for example, 100 installation sites gets exaggerated to 1,000 sites), and misrepresentations about your company's offerings. He has seen distributors drop warranty information so they can charge clients for repairs. Zach says it is just "poor sales leadership to have your distributors translate your materials" because you risk accuracy and misallocate your teams' time – and risk losing your hard-earned trust!

Zach reminds us to look at the costs of bad translation. First, assess the value of the market and then consider the cost of lost effort and revenue if you do it incorrectly. The right professional translator fully understands both languages in the spoken and written formats, as well as the subject matter, and pays close attention to details.

When a $3 million proposal costs $200 to translate, he questions, "Is it worth risking the revenue to save costs on translation?" He has seen too many companies blow opportunities by trying to save costs on translation. In one situation, poor translation by a distributor set the company back two years in their market entry.

Zach also stresses the importance of good verbal language support. In addition to relying on professional translators for written material, he hires interpreters for spoken communications. In the Middle East he can speak English and be understood. But in Latin America and Asia, he hires interpreters to make sure his meaning is clear and delivered in a culturally appropriate manner. In one situation, a distributor made an error and he had to talk to them about it. He told his interpreter, "Do not soften what I am going to say. I am going to be rude." He paid $200 for an interpreter for the meeting and clearly explained what went wrong in the $4 million sale so that the distributor could clearly understand and avoid repeating the mistake.

As a professional sales expert, Zach says that he considers the return on investment on every dollar he spends on growing a market. To build trust and successful global sales, he makes sure to have a strategy, enter the right markets, and hire professionals for accurate communication.

And with that we come full circle in our discussion on how language and culture influence business relationships with international staff, customers, and vendors. Next, we'll expand on Zach's point about optimizing your return on investment by diving deeper into how people are an invaluable resource for global business success.

KEY POINTS TO REMEMBER:

- Get your materials professionally translated for success in global selling.

- Use professional interpreters for important and culturally appropriate verbal conversations.

- Take time to find the right in-country personnel to support your market entry.

Hear Zach's full podcast episode

- https://www.rapporttranslations.com/the-global-marketing-show/global-sales-vs-global-marketing

FUELING GROWTH FROM WITHIN

CHAPTER 11

USE LOCAL EMPLOYEES WISELY

"If a translation is not done well, it can come across as inauthentic and will negatively impact the trust of your potential leads."

—*Randi Roger, Black Box, Senior Product Manager*

I n the last chapter, we discussed the importance of adapting to the local culture, building relationships, and establishing trust. What about working with local employees? On the *Global Marketing Show* (Episode 4), Randi Roger, Senior Product Manager at Black Box,[20] shared how she did not use her local employees efficiently and, as a result, lost business by taking them away from their key job responsibilities.

TRANSLATION OPTIONS

When Randi managed the global marketing team at her former employer, she considered different options for the company translations. Aware of the costs for a professional translation company, she considered other alternatives:

- **Using "Global English"** – As Randi explains, "Saying English is the global language can create negative feelings in individual countries. It comes across as condescending and ethnocentric, resonating negatively toward the brand. It affects everything." So, she quickly determined that relying exclusively on English was not an option.

- **Hiring Inexpensive Bilingual People** – If a translation is not done well, it comes across as inauthentic and negatively impacts the trust of your potential leads, as we learned from Zach Selch in Chapter 10. Randi did not want a series of individuals who lacked the training and experience to provide translations. She did not want to trust the translation to just any bilingual person.

- **Assigning Internal Staff** – Doing translations in-house seemed easier and more efficient. As she and many others thought, "I have Spanish- or French-speaking people already, so why not have them translate the materials?" Randi's company tasked the local marketing people to spend one week a month translating new materials. This strategy seemed to benefit the company with financial savings, high-quality output (since employees understood the material and marketing lingo), and departmental control in knowing who did the translation.

Additionally, Randi found that local people could culturally adapt the content. In Japan, for instance, the employee tasked with translation explained that the concept of *improving the customer experience* simply does not exist because Japanese companies inherently focus on customer service excellence. It's a basic tenet of good business. The marketing campaign to *improve customer experience* needed to be adapted to work in Japan.

REAL COST OF USING EMPLOYEES TO TRANSLATE

Randi admitted that she left the company before she simplified the translation process. In hindsight, she now realizes that the company lost revenue because local employees missed trade shows to translate content. "You have to quantify the cost of that person not doing their job, like covering trade shows, because they are doing translations. If you can hire someone [to translate] for less than what it will cost the person to skip a trade show… those are some of the things to think about when quantifying the cost."

The opportunity cost far outweighed hiring a professional translator. Although using an internal employee worked for them at the time, Randi articulated the lost benefits from not working with a professional translation agency:

- **Centralized effort and time frame** – By using a professional agency, her group could have managed the process while the agency handled the details. While her team focused on designing marketing campaigns, the translation team could translate and adapt the materials to bring efficiency and focus to their efforts.

- **Consistent global messaging** – Although it seemed to save costs by relying on local marketing employees to handle translations, the global message got muddled. When they sent the campaigns to Spain and Latin America, the two local marketing managers did Spanish translations focusing on each local market. This resulted in inconsistent global branding and two different messages for markets that spoke the same language. If they had used an agency, it would have been more cost effective, efficient, consistent, and higher quality. (Note to the reader: for this company, a globalized translation would have made sense. Even for companies that need to localize, it is best to have a coordinated translation strategy across markets.)

- **Consistency of voice** – A good agency assigns experts with language, culture, and subject matter expertise and keeps that translator matched with the company ("linguistic matchmaking"). Randi acknowledged that if an employee left, so did all their knowledge and files about the translations. Professional translators maintain glossaries, translation memories, and archived files for consistency, even if another professional has to step in.

- **High quality** – Randi was lucky that her employees were fully bilingual and produced high-quality work. Yet, other companies shared that employees misunderstood the source content and created inaccurate translations, leading to liability issues. Others admitted that employees purposely changed the message since they thought it "sounded better." When considering all the work it takes to create the original version, why risk quality issues with an untrained, unprofessional translator? Let employees do the job you hired them to do.

- **On-time delivery** – Imagine taking 25% of your work time to do a job that you were not hired to do. Randi's marketing employees, excused from their other responsibilities to the detriment of the company, did get the translations done on time. Yet, other companies ask employees to translate materials in addition to their responsibilities, resulting in delays with both the translations and their regular work. Randi points out that hiring a reputable translation agency means your employees get their work done and you get your translations done – all on time.

- **Document management** – As mentioned above, translation agencies keep archives of projects so that already translated content is available. Employees who do this as a side project do not have glossaries, translation management systems, and document management systems. Plus, if the employee leaves, so do the archives, knowledge, and history.

- **Experienced advice** – A good agency will also share multilingual strategies and discuss best practices for managing multilingual content, allowing you to benefit from industry-wide experience and expertise. Employees without translation experience may not know ways to improve translation management systems.

In Randi's case, using internal employees provided high-quality and timely translations. Yet, she admits that had she stayed at the company longer, she would have changed the process so that her employees could do their job and attend the critical business-related conferences. Hiring a translation agency to streamline the process made sense.

In this chapter we specifically looked at asking international employees to do language and cultural adaptation projects beyond the scope of their business development roles. Consider other atypical tasks that you request local employees handle, just because they are in the local market. Research alternative resources to support those efforts so that your local employees can focus on their jobs, particularly if they are in business development.

KEY POINTS TO REMEMBER:

- Use employees for their assigned tasks even though they may have the knowledge and expertise to translate. The direct costs and lost productivity can be substantial.

- Nurture the relationship with your professional translation company to access suggestions, resources, and services that can help your business grow.

Hear Randi's full podcast episode at

- https://www.rapporttranslations.com/the-global-marketing-show/english-not-the-global-language

CHAPTER 12

IT TAKES A VISION

"Develop a mission that people in all markets innately understand."

—*Andrew Jason, Grand Farm, Director of Ecosystem*

We just learned that utilizing staff for their intended role, not ad hoc tasks, creates efficiency and ultimately saves costs and time. But how do you motivate and rally employees to drive your business forward? When language and cultural differences exist, the best way to motivate everyone is to create a vision and mission statement with universal appeal.

What do you get when you combine agriculture and technology? Sometimes you get a biologically created food patty developed in a lab, and other times you get innovation to increase production of natural foods on farms.

In 2017, Fargo, North Dakota (ND) entrepreneur Barry Batcheller challenged the community to define the region's "major," or the area's specialty, to attract innovation and new businesses to the area. The challenge blossomed into the idea to lean into the region's strong history in agriculture innovation and create a place where stakeholders across the globe could come together to solve the biggest challenges facing agriculture.

Andrew Jason, the Director of Ecosystem at Grand Farm, joined us on *The Global Marketing Show* (Episode 132) to talk about Grand Farm's fast success.

Andrew explained that shortly after Barry posed his challenge, Emerging Prairie, a non-profit focused on energizing communities, created a vision for Grand Farm. After sharing this vision with the community, a local entrepreneur donated land and Microsoft pledged $1.5 million to accelerate the development of the vision. Soon, local business and civic leaders came together to champion the idea.

THINK GLOBAL FROM THE START

By 2024, Grand Farm opened their 590-acre campus just west of Fargo, ND. The developers intentionally designed it as a place to carry forward the mission and vision of solving challenges in agriculture. The campus included land to facilitate demonstration, research, development, and validation of technology with innovators from around the world and an innovation shop to convene this ecosystem, providing opportunities for collision of both collaborators and competition.

This effort, seen as innovative in the post-Covid world, had federal programs watching it for economic development and resiliency. These opportunities highlighted how Grand Farm's Innovation Framework could solve problems not just in agriculture but in any industry. Already, Grand Farm is a:

- Core Partner on awards from the US Economic Development Administration's Good Jobs Challenge and National Science Foundation's Engines Program
- Consortium member of a CHIPS and Science Act, Technology Hub
- Partner with the US Department of Agriculture, Agricultural Research Services
- Partner with the US Small Business Administration

In addition to US government partnerships, Grand Farm partnered with:

1. University of Georgia's College of Agricultural and Environmental Sciences (UGA CAES) to build the UGA Grand Farm, a 250-acre

innovation site located in Perry, Georgia, to serve as the regional hub to support the vision.

2. Deep Valley, an AgTech ecosystem builder in Fukaya City, Japan, to foster international innovation in agriculture.

3. Headwaters Tech Hub to establish a testing site in Bozeman, Montana, to conduct similar operations to those at the Grand Farm Innovation Campus.

At each of these locations, Grand Farm works with the regional ecosystems of growers, commodity groups, and the local agriculture industry to identify the main pain points facing agriculture in each of its regions. From there, Grand Farm pulls in technology and solutions from a global innovation ecosystem to solve for those challenges. Some of the technologies they work in include sensors, drones, robotics, artificial intelligence, biologics, connectivity, and cyber security.

Grand Farm accomplished a tremendous amount in a short time by working with their community and stakeholders to define a vision, and then rallying people across many cultures to buy into their idea.

CLEAR COMMUNICATION

Appropriate communication supported Grand Farm's fast growth: They spoke in English to domestic constituents and shared their translated vision in local languages to non-English-speaking international partners.

The Grand Farm team knew that by not including international partners from the start, they would lose access to the inspiring developments taking place all around the world. And they would miss opportunities to bring the innovations to countries and communities with unique challenges. Grand Farm has found itself in a unique position to be a soft landing spot for international agriculture organizations looking to enter the US market.

Many organizations take decades to build all these relationships. By developing a clear message and using local languages, Grand Farm communicated their vision and built a huge community in only a few years.

A CLEAR VISION DRIVES GROWTH

Many companies that successfully grow internationally also rally around a vision and mission statement that transcends language and culture. Here are some examples:

- Nike's mission: "To bring inspiration and innovation to every athlete in the world."

- Netflix's corporate mission: "To entertain the world."

- Google's mission: "To organize the world's information and make it universally accessible and useful."

- And finally, one of our favorites is Disney's mission: "To make people happy."

Grand Farm also launched with a compelling statement:

"Grand Farm is a network of growers, technologists, corporations, startups, educators, government, and investors working together to solve problems in agriculture with applied technology."

This has resonated with communities, helping to focus progress.

These mission statements work because people can embrace them, no matter their language or culture.

However, sometimes leaders develop a mission statement that they think works everywhere…but it does not. Remember Randi Roger's story in Chapter 11 about a marketing initiative around delivering "service excellence"? When Randi introduced this vision to Japan, the employees looked at her in confusion. She learned that in Japan, a company inherently provides excellent customer service; they could not understand what was unique about that statement. Luckily, Randi and her team heard the concern from the local employees and created a campaign that worked for them.

OVERCOMING CHALLENGES

Of course, even with a strong vision and mission that transcends cultures, there will be challenges. Andrew generously shared some they faced:

- Grand Farm started in North Dakota with a hard-working farming community that grows over 50 crops, including soybeans, wheat, canola, legumes, and oats. They have their own way of communicating and interacting. Each new location that Grand Farm engages has its own local culture, whether in the US or internationally. When working in new locations, they need to retain the global mission while adapting to local needs and preferences. For example, in Georgia the crops differ and the organizational structure within the university entails different management than in North Dakota.

- As we talked about in Chapters 2 and 3, an organization can grow either too quickly or too slowly. The leaders of Grand Farm learned in Japan that developing relationships and trust took longer than expected. This slowed down finalizing their partnerships. But by staying true to their vision and mission, they succeeded and now have strong partnerships in Japan.

- Sometimes people just do not understand each other, which makes it hard to build a partnership. By hiring professional interpreters to communicate, Grand Farm clearly articulated their objectives. This took extra time but helped them avoid misunderstandings.

- Expanding this fast and far takes help. By precisely outlining their goals to trade professionals in their state and federal trade offices, Grand Farm accessed advice and introductions that saved lots of time. In Andrew's case, the North Dakota Trade Office helped immensely. He recommends reaching out to your local trade experts for their advice. (See Chapter 20 and the book Bonus Materials to learn more about how to access your local trade reps.)

The discussion with Andrew about Grand Farm reminded us of how important it is, especially in global business, to set a clear vision and develop a mission that people in all markets innately understand. Testing the mission early in the development with all constituents ensures that it will work long term and across borders.

KEY POINTS TO REMEMBER:

- Develop a clear, universally motivating vision and mission to drive growth.
- Include diverse insights as you develop your vision and mission to increase the likelihood of global success.
- Access resources available from federal and state agencies to help with your export expansion plans.

Hear Andrew's full podcast episode at

- https://www.rapporttranslations.com/the-global-marketing-show/community-innovation-global-agtech

CHAPTER 13

MULTINATIONAL VS. GLOBAL MARKETING

"Always do business with a growth mindset..."

—Liz Fendt, TÜV SÜD, Global Chief Sales and Marketing Director

I n Chapter 6 we heard the story of how a global packaging manufacturer, Conitex Sonoco, unified and centralized their global marketing efforts. Many business leaders share this story of ultimately unifying goals and efforts under a global team to provide brand consistency and motivate cooperation across international groups. These stories cross industries, countries, organizational structure, and leadership values.

Liz Fendt is Global Chief Sales and Marketing Director of TÜV SÜD,[21] which specializes in testing, certification, auditing, and advisory services for different industries. There are only 10 major players in the compliance industry, which ensures safe practices around both goods and services. On the *Global Marketing Show* (Episode 124), she tells us about her journey of transitioning TÜV SÜD from a multinational to a global company.

Prior to her current role, Liz worked in communications and sales and marketing at TÜV SÜD, with a focus on local, regionalized marketing. Inspiration struck the day she analyzed existing collateral and recognized a critical lack of uniformity in marketing materials for the company's global markets; the difference in colors, branding, messaging, and myriad other content and design elements pointed at once to the inefficiencies of duplicated efforts and a missed opportunity for global branding.

Senior management agreed. This led to Liz creating her new role of Global Chief Marketing Director, with the goal of increased efficiencies based on a unified corporate global marketing effort and a cohesive international team.

BUILD A GLOBAL MARKETING TEAM FROM WITHIN

At the start, Liz worked with 120 associates to develop consistent processes and brand/style guidelines. She envisioned the company's German headquarters as the hub of her global marketing "wheel," with satellite offices as its spokes. She deliberately built teams that could move along those spokes to simultaneously integrate the team to accomplish the corporate goals.

A second hub in Singapore followed and Liz saw opportunity there, too – as one global marketing campaign wound down, the next began. She built her teams by elevating associates from within, with intention and according to specialty – pay-per-click, social media, website, document management systems. No associate, role, or team was overlooked, resulting in talented and diverse representation within each group.

Liz's advice on developing global teams with high retention rates: Look for people with a positive outlook that like to solve problems. Two associates who started as interns are now heading global teams. If it's a complex industry, get them in and train them so that they can progress. Energized, excited people with a can-do attitude will thrive with support, contributing new ideas and fostering a healthy work environment.

With that approach, in the first five years and with the same budget, the global marketing team increased leads via the on-hand readiness of standardized, culturally appropriate marketing "in a box." Content and campaigns could be used globally. Liz also consolidated the company's website from 7-10 countries with 42 separate sites, to a single, unified one.

LESSONS LEARNED

Throughout her career, Liz has always turned to her team for inspiration and new ideas. Her best advice is always to do business with a growth mindset and to keep networking – even with people in different fields and industries – because you will always benefit from expertise and diversity of thought.

The TÜV SÜD community of experts spans the globe, and in 2016, Liz co-founded the Global TÜV SÜD Women's Network – a 1,000+ strong network of women across the company – to support and nurture global and local networking, professional mentoring, and role model programs.

Other lessons learned:

- **One size doesn't fit all** – Global marketing for campaigns "in a box" requires a different mix for different markets. Some audiences want white papers while others value human, face-to-face interaction.

- **Start small** – At the start, the company's largest website was the German one. After starting with that site, Liz realized that you should first clean up technology challenges, something more easily done in a smaller market.

- **Stay connected with customers and employees** – Provide a seamless customer journey by understanding how each department affects the customer experience, and that personas come with variables. Similarly, gather your full team periodically for meetings and marketing sessions, and provide channels through which to share information.

Liz adds that technology-driven companies tend to underestimate the value garnered from sales and marketing. A unified global strategy reaps greater benefits when viewed as a "general business propellant" rather than an afterthought. Other common challenges may include:

- **Technology:** It's hard to find tools and IT components for an already robust marketing tech stack.

- **Finding good service providers:** Companies will often claim "global influence" but in effect have only regional coverage with loose partnership and affiliations. One-stop solutions are hard to find.

Today, Liz's 120-person marketing team is a global marketing operation equipped with the support and materials to enter any new market.

The stories in these last few chapters teach us that utilizing employees efficiently and unifying them around a common vision helps drive growth. In the next section you will hear stories and advice for driving growth through external efforts.

KEY POINTS TO REMEMBER:

- Unify global marketing to benefit from better efficiencies and brand consistency.

- Hire motivated employees and promote from within to build a knowledgeable, loyal, and driven team.

- View marketing and sales as a "business propellant" to get the best value from those teams.

Hear Liz's full podcast episode at

- https://www.rapporttranslations.com/the-global-marketing-show/unify-global-marketing-and-succeed

DRIVING GROWTH

CHAPTER 14

UNLEASHING THE POTENTIAL OF TRADE SHOWS

"You don't know what you don't know…"

—*Walter Brooks, Brooksmade Gourmet Foods, CEO*

One way to improve brand recognition and drive sales is by attending trade shows. There are trade shows for all industries focusing on both local and international markets. Finding the right one, and making a key connection, can prove very beneficial – as you are about to hear.

While selling barbeque (BBQ) sauce in the already competitive market of Atlanta, Georgia, in the US presented a challenge, a chance meeting at a local food trade show encouraged one business owner to branch out to an entirely new market, the Middle East. This expansion created millions of dollars in revenue.

Walter Brooks, CEO and Founder of Brooksmade Gourmet Foods,[22] explains on the *Global Marketing Show* (Episode 81) how he first experimented with homemade, all-natural BBQ sauces, ketchups, and marinades in his home kitchen. After many successful tests, he established a food company, developed a brand, trademarked the logo, and subsequently worked with a marketing company to differentiate his products. Starting with local trade shows, farmers markets, and word of mouth, he gradually grew the business through "personal, hand-to-hand combat sales," establishing a strong local fan base in the Atlanta area. Yet he struggled selling BBQ sauce in the already saturated market.

OPPORTUNITY KNOCKS

Luckily, Walter attended a local trade show where a trade representative from the Georgia Department of Economic Development (GDEcD) asked if Walter would consider selling his products to markets outside of the US. Walter immediately jumped on the opportunity. "I thought that was very interesting," he recalls. "I'll go where whoever needs and wants me. If you're that interested, we need to talk!"

GDEcD works under the umbrella of the Southern United States Trade Association (SUSTA). SUSTA guided Walter, introduced him to potential clients and opportunities, and helped him determine the best way to export.

At the same time, Walter started working with a specialist from the Small Business Development Center (SBDC) for the Georgia District who helped him develop a business plan. Fully taxpayer-funded, local SBDC offices are a wildly underutilized resource that offer many services to startups, small, and midsized businesses, including:

- Strategy development and business planning
- Access to capital and financial management
- Personnel administration
- Growth and expansion planning
- Marketing and sales insights
- Export assistance

(We provide contact information for local SBDCs, SUSTA, and GDEcDs in the Bonus Material.)

For Walter, it was an enormous advantage. "You don't know what you don't know," he says. "They helped save me so much money! They set me up with logistics, trade connections, addressed legal issues ... it was a no-brainer for me. After banging my head against a wall and not finding real solutions [in my local market], I was suddenly finding growth!"

In addition to reaching out to local trade representatives and the SBDC, Walter had some other suggestions for exporting success:

1. **Define your target market** – The first steps include determining where you fit by location, demand for product(s), and acceptable price points. Once you determine your target markets, concentrate there.

2. **Go on trade missions** – Walter booked trade missions to specific areas after researching local markets, cultures, and building relationships, with the goal of finding local distributors. He knew that local distributors could save him time and money by delivering his products to their retail suppliers and local markets.

3. **Keep in touch with your trade representative** – While on a trade mission, an SBDC trade rep introduced him to trusted shipping contacts, which made the process easier.

4. **Reach out to US and local consulates** – They have access to many resources that can help with sales, marketing, and partnerships.

TRADE SHOW RELATIONSHIPS

Working with the SBDC and its government contacts, Walter accomplished his goals in half the time he expected. By far the best contacts he made were at the Gulfood Trade Show, the largest food show in the world. By registering his BBQ sauces through the trade show's system and following their onboarding process and advice, he was able to shorten the sales process by making targeted contacts. "If they [the trade reps] like your product, they will walk you through the whole process. They really want your buyers to navigate to you," explains Walter.

Walter's first show happened during the worldwide Covid pandemic, yet he decided to attend anyway. It proved to be the right move! Serious buyers still showed up, and although the show was smaller, being the predominant food show in the world meant it was big enough. The benefit of the reduced size also meant fewer competitors. The US always hosts a large pavilion of tables for small and midsized businesses to display and discuss their trades. Walter recalls, "So many regions came looking for US products and I established two relationships that really stuck out. We hit it off and went to dinner. One happened to be with Warner Brothers, who was building a billion-dollar theme park in the Middle East. They loved our American BBQ sauces and wanted to use them at their theme parks and Ferrari World."

Although that discussion stalled, a chance encounter between a family member working in Dubai and the head of Warner Brothers' Food and Beverage group led to a key meeting with company leadership. From there, Walter was inspired to again pursue the opportunity: "It's all about the relationships you cultivate. I was able to accomplish my four-year plan in two! It took a lot of work building relationships, but many of the distributors I ended up working with I met originally at that show."

GOVERNMENT GUIDANCE

For a small or midsized food or agriculture business trying to break into the international market, the US Economic Development Administration (EDA) provides outstanding benefits and guidance. For other products and services, state trade representatives or local international trade experts from the US Department of Commerce (DOC) can help.

These experts help you research and choose appropriate markets, find distributors, facilitate partnerships, and plan capacity. Walter credited the EDA with providing him with enormous assistance when breaking into the Middle Eastern market. "They helped me cultivate relationships and find a few large distributors from Dubai and Saudi Arabia at that first Gulfood Trade Show, which developed into multimillion-dollar relationships."

EXPORT READINESS

You may already be big enough for global expansion. Walter believes it often relates to production capacity, not revenue. Starting out, he tried to cover domestic and international markets simultaneously, working twice as hard as necessary. After working with the SBDC, he realized that, assuming a company has the manufacturing capacity, a more productive strategy would be to enter the international market early – taking advantage of the free support and subsidies made available by the government for exporters. "It's easier to gain market share by entering the international market this way, because you're emphasizing your natural differences," says Walter. "I'd rather go somewhere where somebody is interested in my products; I can deal with my competitive domestic market later."

The process can be simple:

1. **Do *not* bite off more than you can chew** – Determine how much you can realistically do while you grow. You cannot exactly determine how you will grow, but be honest about your capacity and your capability to deliver – hiding things will spoil vendor relationships over time.

2. **Focus on building relationships** – Avoid transactional interactions and look for genuine, solid relationships. Success comes from creating a foundation built on trust and respect.

3. **View your website from a user perspective** – Keep your customer's viewpoint the focus of your marketing efforts; be user friendly, consistent, and informative. Most customers' initial contact with an organization is online, so if your product information is not online, in the right language, with a compelling reason to buy, prospects will move on.

4. **Incorporate translation and cultural adaptation into your marketing strategy** – Translating your marketing (website, collateral, packaging, labeling, instructions) makes your products easy to understand and use for international customers and prospects. About 70% of websites worldwide are in English, yet only about 5% of the population speaks English natively. Fully 93% of those who don't read English rarely or never visit, or buy, from sites or mobile apps in English.[23]

5. **Provide instant information at trade shows** – Train your staff to identify the right buyers and provide them with the right information effectively. Support conversations with translated marketing materials.

6. **Enable people to buy in their country** – There is more to cross-border purchasing behaviors than language. Privacy, payment methods, delivery, and customs are major components of a localization strategy.

7. **Follow up** – Be ready to reach out and develop relationships with qualified buyers. Chance meetings do not turn into sales – they are the first step in relationship building.

Walter noted that he probably invested about $100,000 to export after all was said and done – and $1 million for R&D, product development, and purchasing. Support from SUSTA paid for travel, trade shows, and research, and after two years the company sold contracts for about $10 million. "A great return on investment! My success came because I kept pushing, regardless of not being 'ready' yet. Your success is action, and action is now. I always advise people to push. Do it now, not later."

Walter did not start out "thinking global from the start," but when the opportunity arose at the local trade show, he took the leap and utilized the resources available to him to drive his growth and success. Walter has definitely not looked back with regret at his decision. He's charging full speed ahead.

KEY POINTS TO REMEMBER:

- Attend trade shows and look for unexpected opportunities.

- Answer the door when global opportunity knocks!

- "Do it now, not later. And, don't be afraid," says Walter.

Hear Walter's full podcast episode at

- https://www.rapporttranslations.com/the-global-marketing-show/
  bbq-sauce-translates-in-dubai

CHAPTER 15

LEVERAGING LINKEDIN

*"If you translate your LinkedIn company page, your
prospects will learn about and trust you."*

—*Viveka von Rosen, Beyond the Dream Board, Keynote
Speaker and LinkedIn Expert*

E very marketer knows the power of social media. No matter the size
of your business, having a social media presence is essential. But
which platform is best for reaching your target audience? A good
place to start is LinkedIn.

LinkedIn is more than just a resume – it's a resource. People from around
the world who want to learn about you, or your company, click on LinkedIn
to find out about your background and skills, and if you are a good fit for
their needs.

OPTIMIZING LINKEDIN FOR ORGANIC GROWTH

Viveka von Rosen, a Keynote Speaker, LinkedIn expert, and author of
LinkedIn Marketing: An Hour a Day and 101 Ways to Rock Change, spoke on
the *Global Marketing Show* (Episode 15) about how global companies can
best present themselves on LinkedIn.

To start, Viveka recommends making sure that your company page clearly
describes your organization and includes links to your website. Then, set up

translated pages in the languages spoken by your key markets. She cautions you to set the pages up correctly – many companies create separate LinkedIn company pages for each language, rather than having a single company page in multiple languages. This results in lost global reach. With LinkedIn, it is easy to add multilingual versions of your company page through the "manage languages" tool. Just remember to load high-quality translations, as this could be a prospect's first impression of your company.

Here are the steps to add languages to your company LinkedIn page:

1. Navigate to your company page and "View as admin".

2. Scroll on the left panel and click "Edit page".

3. Click on the left navigation to "Manage languages".

4. Click + Add a language.

5. Select your language.

6. Drop in your high-quality translation for your tagline and description.

ADDING LANGUAGE TO LINKEDIN COMPANY PAGE

Edit   ✕

	Manage other languages for page name and description. Learn more
Header	
Page info	+ Add a language
Buttons	
Home	

Language	Name	Tagline	Description	Actions
English (English) (Default)	Beyon d th...	My experti...	Viveka von Rosen, a celebrated LinkedIn expert, bestselling author, and...	✏

Featured
About
Overview
Interested talent
Workplace
Commitments
Locations
Leads
Lead gen form

Manage languages

Next, educate and involve your employees. Organizations benefit from training employees to set up personal LinkedIn pages, link them to the company page, and post.

Viveka can teach your employees how to approach LinkedIn with the right mindset, use appropriate manners, and convey the best image of themselves. When employees create a personal brand and effectively use the platform, they connect with their prospects, clients, and network to stay visible and helpful – all benefits to the individual *and* their employer.

Let's look at her suggestions and how to adapt them for global marketing:

- **Ask bilingual employees to create profiles in multiple languages** and link their pages to the company's original and translated pages. Just like company pages, LinkedIn offers tools to create multilingual pages for individuals.

- **Create content for employees in different languages.** This makes it easier for employees to find and share information with their connections in their preferred language(s).

- **Ensure that content is culturally appropriate** and sounds pure human in all marketing interactions on social media, especially in this day of AI-generated content.

- **Train employees how to create appropriate posts** and encourage them to post in their native languages.

- **Assign specific employees to post content in their native language on company pages.** Content does not automatically feed from the main page, so unless a person manually transfers, it will not happen. Assigning people to post important and popular posts in all organization languages increases engagement.

- **Facilitate conversations between departments and cultures.** To have a cohesive message everyone can rally around, "Marketing and sales teams should take each other to lunch and ask about departmental and cultural differences and what they can both do to help," says Viveka. "What nuances should be changed? What should be avoided? Which differences are cultural versus language-specific?"

- **Teach sales representatives effective ways to create and engage in social posting.** By creating and posting their own content rather than relying on marketing, reps develop their personal brand in their native language to engage prospects. This benefits everyone when done appropriately.

Viveka stresses that if you encourage employees to create their own posts, make sure to set guidelines for what is appropriate: personal stories that do not offend or complain, work stories that align with your culture and brand, current events (non-political), and content that is not embarrassing, confidential, or inappropriate. Best practice is to create a policy about social media posting and share it during new employee onboarding and in your employee manual. Remember to include your international employees in the training and encourage them to post in their native language.

CONSIDER LINKEDIN PAID ADVERTISING

On the *Global Marketing Show* (Episode 53), AJ Wilcox, Founder of B2Linked,[24] an online agency specializing in LinkedIn ads, explains: "When I first began creating LinkedIn ads in the early days of LinkedIn, my digital marketing firm quickly discovered that 100% of the leads we were getting came from LinkedIn! I decided to start my own business [helping others with LinkedIn ads] because I had gotten so many great results and was so passionate about the work."

AJ clarifies that while Facebook advertisers cannot directly target the decision maker, LinkedIn advertising can. "If you consider the lead scoring grading tool, BANT (Budget, Authority, Need, Timing)," he says, "keyword searching via Google or Safari [or Facebook] will produce strong results on need and timing, but you do not necessarily know if someone has the budget or authority."

Yet developing a coordinated strategy around LinkedIn, Facebook, and Google ads optimizes an organization's outreach, since the platforms work together to allow an organization to retarget leads to give them another impression of your brand. Since LinkedIn ads are more expensive than Facebook or Google, many people begin their online advertising efforts there. Ultimately, using Facebook and LinkedIn together provides the most competitive strategy: "They really work well together. They should not be viewed as competing but as complementary tactics."

From the beginning, LinkedIn ads have been more expensive, starting at $2 per click. Facebook and Google, on the other hand, began with low prices ($.05) and the level of competition grew organically. This holds true in global markets, too.

Since LinkedIn is based in the US, its North American market grew quickly and became expensive; now many of its per-click charges are $8-$12, yet in South America the costs may be only $1-2 per click. Western and Eastern Europe also have different rates, still lower than the US.

AJ suggests trying international LinkedIn ads, targeting buyers by language or by country for lower costs. Since LinkedIn ads are relatively expensive in any market, "They should provide a real benefit, be a lead magnet," he adds. And, when creating global ads for LinkedIn, Facebook, or Google, AJ stresses the importance of accurately translated and culturally adapted keywords so people find you. "Sometimes teams are moving too fast and cutting corners and they use Google Translate, which can cause real problems." He reminded us again that grammatical errors, bad translations, and incorrect idioms insult readers and can destroy a brand image for years. Do not let your LinkedIn advertising make a bad first impression.

Here are some of his tips for global online advertising:

- **Take advantage of digital keyword research and associated costs.** Google, for example, lists the competition level for keywords, making it easier to start with less expensive search terms. Develop a good

English keyword list and then have the words professionally translated and researched for search results.

- **Limit spending by targeting cheaper online traffic.** Consider going global to start and test advertisements.

- **Pay attention to online traffic and time of day.** Sometimes, online clicks may be more expensive depending on the time of day. Play with global time zones.

- **Look for specific targeting traits.** LinkedIn, for example, can target business travelers and expats living abroad – a smaller, defined market with the potential for huge returns.

- **Target your ad campaigns by language.** With LinkedIn you do not pay unless someone clicks on a link, so try campaigns in multiple languages.

- **Translate your company page on LinkedIn in multiple languages.** With high-quality translation of your company page, your prospects can learn about and develop trust in you.

It's an old, outdated notion that "English is the global language," says AJ. "Companies should make the effort to align with buyers and try to speak their language. It is simply arrogant *not* to."

Social media is powerful and companies that use it wisely see the returns. Whether you decide to use paid advertising, organic outreach, or a combination of both, remember to translate and culturally adapt your content to connect, engage, and delight all audiences!

KEY POINTS TO REMEMBER:

- Show LinkedIn company and personal pages in multiple languages so that you connect with your international audience.
- Make sure you have quality translation on your pages.
- Increase your reach across LinkedIn by training employees on how to engage in company appropriate ways.
- Drive leads with less expensive paid advertising to target international clients.

Hear Viveka's full podcast episode at

- https://www.rapporttranslations.com/the-global-marketing-show/linkedin-in-multiple-languages

Hear AJ's full podcast episode at

- https://www.rapporttranslations.com/the-global-marketing-show/53-global-linkedin-ads-more-affordable

CHAPTER 16

CONNECTING WITH PEOPLE

"Experiential selling is what matters now, not the product."

—*Barbara (Babs) Ryan, Sparks Worldwide, President*

U ltimately, every business's goal is to connect to people. Whether selling earrings or providing marketing services, every sale is between people.

Of all the human gestures, a smile is the only one recognized worldwide. Smiling puts people at ease and makes them more open to engage with you. Yet knowing how to smile in a culturally appropriate way is important, as sometimes smiling too soon or too big can cause issues! The Japanese, for instance, view women who laugh with an open mouth as garish and rude. As discussed in Chapters 8 and 9, taking the time to understand these subtle cultural differences affects your success in international business.

EXPERIENTIAL SELLING

Babs Ryan, President of Sparks Worldwide[25] and an international marketing expert who has traveled and worked in 96 countries, explains further on the *Global Marketing Show* (Episode 46): "The best international marketing is about people and connecting them. Nike is brilliant at it. The original idea behind ***Nike***+ was to create a shoe monitor to record your steps. But they found that people ran more if they ran with others and would then buy more running-related products. So, they developed an app to connect people so they could find ways to run together based on location and running level. They connected human beings. That's what it's all about: selling people to people and figuring out how to connect people to one another."

In addition, rather than trying to reach every consumer worldwide, Nike determined that they could target just twelve international markets with certain themes or sports. Those larger markets influenced other smaller markets. By emphasizing how and who used their products rather than the products themselves, they honed a highly successful strategy that focused on why people use their products, what they feel about them, and how they connect when using them.

"Experiential selling is what matters now, not the product," explains Babs. "If you think about it, all customer experiences are experiential. How does wearing that shoe or riding that motorcycle make you feel?"

Nike is not the only company to capitalize on experiential selling. REI and Orvis both began offering experiences for customers to travel with like-minded people, encouraging use of their products for the trips. Airbnb International added advice and links to connect travelers to activities and information near the chosen location once they booked a stay. These features promoted additional travel experiences based on human connections, not just places to stay. Meetup, an online platform, offers ways to meet people anywhere in the world through affinity groups, local networks, and shared interests. "This is what matters most right now – connecting people to one another, especially in international marketing," notes Babs. By encouraging people to connect to each other through shared interests, companies no longer need to focus strictly on the products; they will sell themselves.

TIPS FOR CONNECTING TO PEOPLE

Here are Babs' 3 tips for building relationships while going global:

1. UNDERSTAND LOCAL CUSTOMS

When creating marketing plans and tools, communicating in the local language is important, but it's not just about the words – it's about how words make you *feel*. Babs also noted that it is important not to rely completely on Google Translate (or AI programs). As we discussed in Chapter 7, these automated programs are unable to give you a sense of the cultural norms of a specific place or the behaviors and habits of a particular country or population. "The trick," says Babs, "is to know the culture and the 'why' behind what people [your consumers] do. Go to people that know the why. Get experts from those [sources]."

Babs uses the example of selling jewelry – specifically, engagement rings. In the US, women tend to wear their rings all the time. Yet, in China, women do not wear an engagement ring every day, reserving them for special occasions. In France, many women prefer colored stones. Researching differences and adapting your marketing to local customs and behavioral norms becomes critical in marketing your goods or services.

2. STAY CURIOUS - LEARN FROM DIVERSITY OF THOUGHT AND BEHAVIOR

Traveling and having experiences beyond your normal routine gives you insight into global cultures. Babs described a funny experience she had in Iran while waiting for bread in a bakery line: "There I was, wearing a burka with sneakers on…and a man motioned for me to go ahead. I motioned, 'No, no, it's ok', and then more and more men began doing the same thing. When a woman walked right past me to the head of the line, I couldn't figure out what was going on. Turns out, I was in the men's line! There was a separate line for women and men. But I never would have known [about a particular custom like that]!" Without this experience, Babs would not have understood this local custom that could influence marketing decisions.

In the UK she found that "the level of innovation and love of change (at least within the advertising industry [where I had been working]) far exceeds that in the US." She suggested that finding teammates from UK advertising companies could increase a company's innovation dramatically.

Whereas in Kenya, in 2010, over 70% of the Kenyan population used M-PESA (M for mobile and PESA is Swahili for money), an early form of mobile money transfer, payments, and micro-financing services, long before the rest of the world caught on. She remembers, "They were basically texting money, without extra apps – just using the phone itself as an application. It all goes back to looking at behavior and different ways of doing things. We need to be open to the notion that there may be better, easier ways to do things than the ways we are accustomed to."

Without extensive travel and observation, it may be difficult to understand cultural differences. Yet having a local expert to coach you about various norms and practices helps you avoid errors and capture the cultural nuances in your company communications.

Babs recommends that you always ask these questions as you travel (or to your expert):

- Why do your customers use your products?
- Is the answer the same across markets?
- How can you connect consumers to increase your product/services use?

3. THINK GLOBAL FROM THE START

Babs reiterated the importance of thinking globally from the start, particularly in product development. Rather than focusing solely on the technology or product, think about what the product **does** and how it helps consumers. A global mindset allows you to find broader applications for a product and create innovative ways to connect to your global end users – to people who want connection and belonging. Too often, innovators develop products that can only be used in the home country because they did not consider cross-cultural sales from the start.

Although it may seem difficult to understand global markets and local cultures, according to the US Department of Commerce, "Exporting can be profitable for businesses of all sizes. On average, sales grow faster, more jobs are created, and employees earn more than in non-exporting firms."[26] Companies that develop and market products with global end users in mind succeed faster. When Nike started selling internationally, they identified twelve key markets and achieved enormous international success in these limited geographies. Now, they are in 170 countries. At the start of every initiative, assign a person to champion the global campaign, focus on global marketing, and over time, you will succeed.

KEY POINTS TO REMEMBER:

- Sell your product or service by connecting with people to create a sense of belonging.
- Learn about the local culture and customs to connect with customers on a more meaningful level.
- Assign a champion for each target global market.
- Think global from the start (have you heard this enough yet?!).

Hear Babs' full podcast episode at

- https://www.rapporttranslations.com/the-global-marketing-show/46-88-countries-counting

CHAPTER 17

BUILDING GLOBAL COMMUNITIES

"You will need to have people on the ground (or good translators to advise you) who understand the culture and language in that particular environment."

—Dani Weinstein, Community Strategist, Builder and Advisor

I n the last chapter, Babs Ryan explained the importance of building connections between consumers to build awareness and sales. She mentioned Nike, Orvis, Airbnb, and other companies that found great success in doing this. These companies understood the importance of connection early on and developed robust programs. As this type of marketing exploded, companies started hiring "community engagement specialists" to focus on encouraging and rewarding interaction among customers, building virtual communities, and integrating online and in-person experiences to create strong social interactions to drive customer satisfaction, loyalty, and, ultimately, sales.

Dani Weinstein, a Community Strategist, Builder, and Advisor[27] who has worked at Kaltura, SAP, DOMO, and HP, joined us on the *Global Marketing Show* (Episode 49) to share his expertise on starting, building, and expanding communities around the world that speak different languages and have rich cultural diversity.

BUILDING A COMMUNITY

Dani explains that companies such as Dell and Microsoft, in addition to the ones Babs spoke about, started doing this over 20 years ago, even before the rise of the internet. And we can learn from them.

Before launching a community, it is wise to get senior leadership to buy into this strategy, as it is a longer-term initiative, and then set goals for the next three to five years. Then, follow these steps:

- Research where your customers hang out online – they may be posting or interacting on various websites or within online forums and chat rooms.

- Determine who uses your product(s) and what they are talking about.

- Create a place for dialogue and engagement.

- Start small. Perhaps create several online "rooms" with a narrow focus on key topics that can later be expanded into larger "rooms" or verticals.

- Let customers drive the topics and content. You can supplement or augment later with company content.

- Create an environment where customers feel comfortable. There should be a balance between customer- and company-generated content.

- Identify knowledgeable and service-oriented employees to follow the interactions and interact appropriately.

Dani notes that, typically, only about one-third of an organization's customers engage in a community. A small percentage of that population will look for some sort of recognition; the key is to curate these customers over time because they can be great influencers, content providers, and participants in forums and online chat rooms. Recognize them on leaderboards and eventually you may be able to use them in conferences or for speaking engagements.

"The trick is to find the right spaces and platforms, because [platforms such as] Facebook (or Meta) ultimately control their boards," Dani explains.

HubSpot and Entrepreneurs Organization (EO) developed their own platforms to control engagement and decrease the risk of another platform changing access or policies that could affect the communities. However, organizations may choose a third-party platform (such as Facebook, Slack, WhatsApp, Feverbee.com, or The Community Club) to avoid the tech development needed for a proprietary platform.

EXPANDING A COMMUNITY

Once you start a community, it takes consistent effort to grow active engagement. As you bring your community together, remember to include your global customers for faster growth, more engagement, and deeper insights. This requires understanding the differences in your global customers' culture and language and finding new methods for communicating and connecting. To do this, consider the following questions:

1. Where are your customers based?
2. Who is joining the communities?
3. What are they creating or offering online?
4. Who are they engaging with?
5. How are they engaging with your organization?
6. What languages do they use to communicate with one another, or as consumers?

"In general, you need several thousand people as occasional customers to truly create a community. Out of those users, a smaller portion will be engaged users and from that group, perhaps 50 will be power users," notes Dani. "There are always costs associated with creating a community: information technology, personnel, and understanding the language. And you need to be able to justify those costs."

HANDLING LANGUAGE IN YOUR COMMUNITY

Adding languages to your virtual forums or online communications expands access to your community. When you have enough active and appropriate users, professional translators help with community engagement and connection. Although some companies may try using Google Translate, the quality is not good enough to engage participants; ultimately, they may leave.

"You will need to have people on the ground (or good translators to advise you) who understand the culture and language in that particular environment," emphasizes Dani. He adds, "Before you begin to create marketing materials or campaigns, you need to work with that team to get the pulse of the market and customer expectations to determine what will succeed in that market."

As an organization grows internationally, remember that not everyone thinks or perceives things the same way. "I remember when I was at Hewlett Packard making a presentation in the Czech Republic," he recalls. "We were using an American, 1950s-style brochure, and slides using the analogy of burgers and fries. They did not get it at all. We had to change the analogy to Czech pilsner and meatballs!"

Once you establish a multilingual community, you will want to support it with professionally translated corporate materials, such as your websites, support materials, and user manuals. Dani explains that the most important advice is not to approach the process piecemeal. He suggests:

- Have a strategy about what you will translate and when.

- Think through the buyer's journey to determine appropriate content for each stage.

- Start small and then support your community as it grows by expanding translation or engaging active, native-speaking clients.

THINK GLOBAL FROM THE START

As we heard from Babs in the last chapter and many others, Dani also reminds us to. . .think global from the start! Many companies forget about growing globally until it is too late – for example, after they developed their technology incorrectly or lost out to faster moving competitors. As we mentioned before, organizations from smaller countries – Israel, Sweden, or Belgium for example – think global from the start because they must. They have a smaller domestic market, so to succeed they must continually consider larger markets.

Dani explains the opportunity: "With today's technology, a company's reach and markets are boundless," he notes. "They can have customers anywhere in the world. They have multi-language, multi-market views. This provides a clear advantage for these organizations." The key to building successful global communities, he reiterates, is to continually modify, iterate, and adapt communications to increase brand awareness and customer loyalty.

KEY POINTS TO REMEMBER:

- Build communities around your product or service to connect people in a meaningful way.

- Include international customers by providing translated content or culturally adapted campaigns to engage everyone in your community.

- We'll say it again: Think global from the start!

Hear Dani's full podcast episode at

- https://www.rapporttranslations.com/the-global-marketing-show/49-global-community-building

TAKING THE LEAP

CHAPTER 18

STARTING...

"People buy differently in different countries and different cultures."
—*Ed Marsh, Ed Marsh Consulting, Founder*

I n the prior chapters, we shared great stories and advice from a variety of global marketing professionals. But you may still be wondering, "Where do I start?" Let's take a look at some practical and intentional steps you can take to expand your business.

"In Germany, a process engineer in manufacturing goes through a very technical process to determine exactly where something is going wrong and what tool or piece could fix the problem. Yet in the US, engineers address problems in order to achieve desired outcomes. These two approaches result in very different cultural strategies for introducing or bringing a product or service to international markets," explains Ed Marsh, from Ed Marsh Consulting,[28] on the *Global Marketing Show* (Episode 2). "Often, the way in which purchasing happens depends on a buyer's role. In some situations, there are specific processes for how things are purchased. I call this 'sociological transcreation differences.'"

Although global expansion may seem challenging due to language and cultural issues, companies do it every day. Let's round up some final suggestions to inspire you to try, because the rewards far outweigh the challenges.

ORGANIC INTERNATIONAL GROWTH

A huge advantage of international selling is the ability to track website traffic and user location. This limits the amount of research needed to choose new markets. By monitoring your website metrics, you can see where you already have traction. When you notice significant numbers of users from a certain country, target those buyers organically. Either create a translated landing page or a smaller version of your website called a microsite and optimize it for search (SEO) with researched and translated keywords to attract more of those buyers. Companies that measure and test new markets through their website expand internationally without a major commitment.

Often, rather than paying attention to website metrics, companies pursue English-speaking markets simply because they speak the language. This is a huge mistake! Why? Because your domestic competitors typically target the exact same markets and there may not be a demand for your product/service there. Instead, Ed recommends:

1. Track your website traffic and inquiries.

2. Monitor pipeline deals and where they originate.

3. Measure which deals close or drop due to language issues.

4. Determine which deals close with the least amount of conflict.

By analyzing these criteria, the data will point to those markets most likely to succeed.

ANTICIPATING ERRORS WHEN EXPANDING GLOBALLY

As we have noted repeatedly, the process of doing business in other countries and markets differs in a variety of ways. It is important to understand and accept those variations. "Cultural differences will often impact how things are interpreted," Ed emphasizes. Sure, some differences are due to people being people, varying time zones, or fatigue, but legitimate cross-cultural challenges will arise. Remembering these key points will let you work through them:

- **Accept that you will make mistakes** – Do your research in advance as much as possible. You will never avoid mistakes entirely, just accept that things will go wrong and learn to adapt. Often, the most common challenges center around foreign currency, logistics, export issues, legal challenges, and corruption.

- **Adapt** – Rather than seeing failure when mistakes happen, view them as opportunities to learn and adapt to the market. Companies that succeed continually monitor and change when they do not get their desired results.

- **Outsource to experts** – Don't be afraid to outsource. Payroll, for instance, is quite complicated – so outsource it! "My advice," says Ed: "Find experts to help. Get referrals either from people you know or from the Department of Commerce. Don't assume that you have to sell cheaply. And remember that the purchasing process may not be the same as you are accustomed to." Build your team to support your efforts.

- **Grow incrementally** – Worldwide access to the internet contributed to a dramatic change in how companies pursue international business. Now, companies can pursue leads and inquiries as they come through their websites, rather than trying to tackle an entire market at once. "Let the market guide you, rather than the other way around," notes Ed. If you follow your traffic, inquiries, deals in the pipeline, closed deals, and most successful closings, you can determine high demand areas and build a comprehensive market presence based on actual information.

- **Ask questions** – The most repeated advice we hear from guests and clients is to "stay curious." When you do not naturally understand a local culture, language, or business climate, you can always ask. People around the world want to be seen, heard, accepted, and understood. By saying, "Out of curiosity…" and then asking your question, you diffuse tensions and open the door to real engagement.

Beginning to launch or expand your business globally can be a daunting task, but it does not need to be. Think of this as an exciting adventure and take advantage of all the resources available to you – both governmental as well as from other individuals that have gone before you. They will be happy to share their experiences and advice. Be strategic, but don't be afraid to go big. Remember to do your research to determine what your potential buyers want most and to understand the nature of your market. Most importantly, take the time to truly understand the culture and cultural issues surrounding any new markets that you are considering.

Remember, what you initially may consider a disadvantage in your lack of knowledge about a particular place or culture ultimately may help you as you move forward. And. . .always stay curious!

AS YOU TAKE THE LEAP, REMEMBER:

- Grow organically and intentionally based on your current metrics and what works.
- Adapt and learn from mistakes while continuing to move forward.
- Stay curious and enjoy the journey.

Hear Ed's full podcast episode at

- https://www.rapporttranslations.com/the-global-marketing-show/machine-translation-debate

CHAPTER 19

MOVING GRACEFULLY FROM LOCALIZED TO GLOBALIZED

"Don't be afraid, even if it sounds daunting."

—Patrick Nunes, Rotary International, Director of
Global Communications and Design

G rowth is not easy. Just as a child goes through developmental stages, so does an organization. And just as you might reach out to fellow parents or read books or articles to guide you through that process, having the right tools or partner to support your organizational growth can make a major difference in helping you achieve your goals.

Ideally, an organization's global communications strategy should be integrated into the overall strategic vision and business processes, incorporating and valuing languages and culture wherever it does business. Yet, too often communications and language translation are an afterthought.

The story of Rotary International is an older one but still a great example of a large, global organization that grew successfully from a localized, "reactive" communications group to a truly global, or "transparent," communications organization. Using the Localization Maturity Model (LMM) developed by CSA Research[29] is a great way to think about a company's developmental translation stages.

LOCALIZATION MATURITY PROCESS

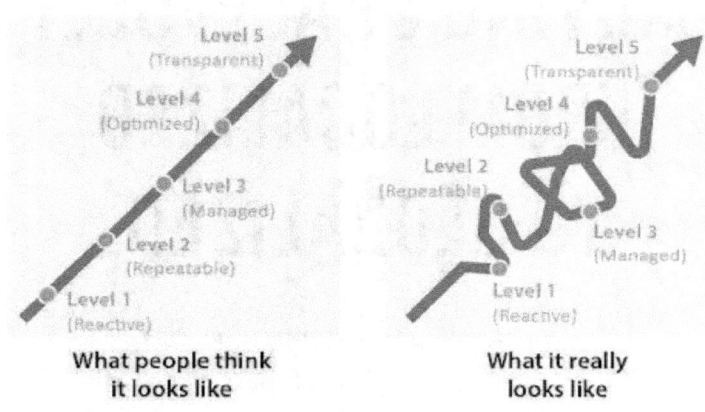

HOW DID ROTARY INTERNATIONAL DO IT?

Founded in 1905, Rotary International began as a group of businessmen who met to network and socialize, adding in humanitarian projects as they went. Today they are 35,000 worldwide clubs strong, "exchanging ideas and connecting to take action and create lasting change." About ten years ago, they realized they had an image and positioning problem. Their communications department originally sent US English-based materials to a "translation needs department," which used a mixed, reactive (level 1) process for translating materials. By 2009, their in-house workflow management system was already obsolete. Although they had a basic translation system, they had no maintenance or quality controls in place. Sometimes translations worked, yet often materials and messages were culturally inappropriate.

ADDING VALUE

"We were really under a rock," explains Patrick Nunes, Rotary's Director of Global Communications and Design, on the *Global Marketing Show* (Episode 17). "We were probably at a level 2...when I arrived. We had some processes but no strategy or formal process." Work was getting done, but not efficiently. As Patrick's department grew, their need for a workflow management system and new technology became increasingly evident. Gradually, by 2011-12, they began moving from a level 2 to a level 3: "We started to look at our role differently, getting more included in corporate-wide conversations and positioning our department as more than just service providers. We were adding value to the conversation and talking about quality." In 2011-12 they developed a quality assurance program: "We now had a seat at the table, but not in a robust manner." Although they were still considered a "translation" group, they were gaining more visibility. But they still knew nothing about the CSA Research LMM curve.

THE TRANSFORMATION

In 2015, a new chief communications officer came on board. During a listening tour with him, Patrick suggested that the translation department could play a greater role, serving as a strategic partner for communications on a global scale: "We had the talent, robust teams like communications and PR, and groups were starting to use social media, but there were no processes around it." But Patrick realized that with a little training they could teach internal teams to think about localization from a broader perspective: "We could transform the copy-editing team, for instance, to look at voice and tone in messaging." English needed to become more global in tone, throughout. "I knew we could get there if we thought about what we wanted to accomplish and the milestones. This was going to be a transformation."

INVOLVING LEADERSHIP

Fortunately, the chief communications officer supported the suggestion. Once Patrick pitched the idea and corporate leadership bought in, the challenge was figuring out how to bring the idea to life. Reaching out to key players who could help, Patrick went to HR for assistance. Together, they recruited people to help him guide the change, capitalizing on and preserving the talent they already had. They created process tracks and considered how to best implement technology, realizing that their team was swamped in translation. The trick became empowering people to do more. Most importantly, Patrick understood that in order to create change they would have to examine the operational side of their department – how work got done and by whom – and how they could facilitate the process through technology.

By 2016 they created a two-year plan with specific milestones to look at processes, technology, professional development, and outsourcing. Before making any investments or changes, they had to examine their internal processes. When people told Patrick, "You can't put a process around creative," he replied, "watch me!" Within nine months they mapped all their functions – from design to interpretation, copy-editing, and localization. They found:

- Lack of insight into how long it took to get projects done
- Haphazard and inconsistent processes
- Redundant steps that could be automated using technology

They realized that outlining and color-coding the workflow could determine how to use technology to improve processes or eliminate steps. They knew that they wanted to use technology to save time, increase productivity, and integrate it corporate-wide by having employees work more productively. They just had to make the case for it.

After mapping everything, they recommended:

1. Apply process improvements as identified during the mapping process.

2. Acquire a new workflow management system.

3. Document and set clear guidelines about how to work with their team.

4.   Implement machine translation and translation memory to alleviate time and expedite turnaround in internal teams.

KEYS TO A SUCCESSFUL GLOBAL COMMUNICATIONS CHANGE

Patrick understood that to become a truly global communications department and strategic partner of the organization, they needed a clear, well-defined vision of where they wanted to be. He and his team thought through all the elements and developed a specific plan. Looking back on the process, his advice is: "Don't be afraid, even if it sounds daunting." To avoid shock during the adventure, keep in mind the following warnings:

WARNING #1: CHANGE IS MESSY

Do not underestimate the steps involved in a change management effort and how messy change can be: it will be! But it is worth it. With the right people in place, your chances of succeeding and sustaining that change are much greater.

WARNING #2: STAKEHOLDERS ARE VITAL BUT CHALLENGING

It can be tough to convince stakeholders that change is worth it, especially when they "feel" productive and accomplished. In Rotary's case, with a little convincing the chief communications officer believed in the vision and advocated it to the CEO and CTO. Be prepared to have thick skin and a clear, repetitive message about the benefits of the change.

WARNING #3: DON'T UNDERESTIMATE PROCESS

By taking time (and lots of it) to analyze your processes and find the broken parts, you will have clarity on the issues. Once you find the issues and communicate them, you might need to break the processes further to achieve the improvements you envision. Sometimes continuing "as is" may restrict you from making improvements. As Patrick notes, "I look at 'process' with affection. It can truly help. But it does not happen overnight."

While Rotary International had the size and funding to build an internal team to grow their global communications efforts, some companies may not have the resources to do it internally. At times, it is worth reaching out to your translation agency to seek their support to get results that will align with your organizational strategy.

Patrick confessed that it took years to convert Rotary from English-centric to globally focused. Yet the time and effort paid off. No matter what country you visit, you hear a consistent brand message that has helped Rotary unite and grow.

KEY POINTS TO REMEMBER:

- Set a vision for your global communications.
- Outline your processes to see where you can improve.
- Build a team to support your vision for clear communications in any language.

Hear Patrick's full podcast episode at

- https://www.rapporttranslations.com/the-global-marketing-show/us-centric-to-globally-oriented

CHAPTER 20

HELPFUL RESOURCES ARE AVAILABLE

"Exporting is the secret to fast business growth!"

—*Wendy MacKenzie Pease, Rapport International, Owner*

I n prior chapters, we mentioned support programs and resources available to help companies take the leap into exporting. These options range in price from no cost, reimbursable, to fee-based. It's the free and low cost – yet valuable – opportunities that we focus on in this chapter. In Episode 144 of the *Global Marketing Show*, co-author Wendy Mackenzie Pease, host of the show and President of Rapport International,[30] serves double duty as both host and guest as she shares information about helpful resources.

Note: *For even more information, you will find links to "Bonus Material" and "Special Offers" in the final chapter where you can access information such as: federal and state advisors, supportive organizations, learning resources, and valuable Special Offers from trusted service providers. The links take you to continually updated information online. Please, share any helpful sources you find with the authors for inclusion in the Bonus Material or introductions to your trusted advisors interested in including a Special Offer.*

SEIZE THE OPPORTUNITY

Despite the clear benefits of trading internationally, less than 5% of America's 30 million companies export. That tiny percentage of businesses exported over $1.5 billion in 2021. So why do so few US companies export? An SBA report cites the following feedback from US exporters:

- 45% cite a lack of knowledge of the export process

- 28% face regulatory barriers

- 20% have uncertainty about being paid

- 14% cite the costs of exporting

The survey also showed that "53% of non-exporting businesses would be interested in exporting in the future if these barriers were addressed."[31]

On the flip side, 93% of international small businesses export to an average of 13 to 35 marketplaces worldwide. If you think about smaller countries like Belgium or Israel, it makes sense – they are looking for larger markets. Yet, India is notable for the 58% of small business sales via cross-border trade. In fact, the *Economic Time*s reported in July 2023 that "small businesses from emerging economies are excelling in international trade, outperforming advanced market counterparts and net exporters."[32]

Free resources for US companies exist because the US imports so much more than it exports, keeping the balance of trade perpetually off balance. By supporting companies that export, the federal and state governments help mitigate the imbalance for a healthier economy.

FEDERAL GOVERNMENT RESOURCES

The US Department of Commerce (DOC) houses the International Trade Administration (ITA) with an office in every state, offering services such as:

- Economic and demographic information from around the world

- Product classification database for export control information

- Introductions to international, in-market trade officials

- Commercial diplomacy to overcome obstacles for success

- A global market finder to identify good export markets

- Export control information and support

- Trade data on ports, values of products, and import regulations

- Gold Key Service (fee-based) to provide matchmaking appointments with pre-qualified prospects

US Embassies and consulates based in countries around the world fall under the DOC and can assist with market entry. Contact the US Embassy's commercial attaché for help with business expansion and contact the consulate for personal help with travel, visas, documentation, and passports.

STATE GOVERNMENT SUPPORT

US companies **who do not know where to start** can look to a local US Export Assistance Center (USEAC). With offices in every state supported by the US Department of Commerce, the Small Business Development Centers (SBDC), the EXIM Bank, and the Small Business Association (SBA), USEACs help small companies:

- Access capital for expansion

- Develop and launch new technologies

- Improve export business planning, strategy, and operations

- Attain financial and human resource stability across markets

- Initiate global marketing and sales, including translation and cultural adaptation

- Expand digital marketing reach

- Provide introductions to federal and state personnel at international offices

In addition, in most states the USEACs are the organizations that manage the State Trade Expansion Program (STEP) grants that offset international and business development and marketing related costs for small businesses. The local USEACs work closely with the federal trade office so that small and midsized companies can access financial support and introductions to qualified partners, in-country distributors, and experienced service providers.

DISTRICT EXPORT COUNCILS (DECs)

The National Association of District Export Councils (NADEC) increases awareness and understanding of the importance of exports to the US economy through education, legislative outreach, and engagement with local DECs. In each state, local chapters support the national mission by mentoring businesses, identifying financing options, advocating for trade policy and legislation, supporting USEACs, and providing education about exporting.

WORLD TRADE CENTERS

With over 300 World Trade Centers (WTCs) around the world in almost 90 countries, the centers belong to an association that focuses on stimulating trade and investment opportunities for property developers, economic development agencies, and international businesses looking to expand. The service offerings, the activity level, and the local reach varies quite a bit by location. In some states, the local WTC serves as a connector to the State USEAC and US ITA, whereas in other states the WTC is the driving force in educational and networking events, managing STEP grants and trade missions. It is worth connecting with your WTC to learn how to work optimally with them.

GLOBAL TRADE COMMUNITIES, ASSOCIATIONS, AND NETWORKS

After venturing into global business, you will soon learn that the world is small. After joining a few organizations focused on exporting and trade, you will run into some of the same people. There are Chambers of Commerce that bring together the home country and local community;

executive groups that focus on managing international companies; women or minorities in trade organizations; airport-seaport/logistics associations; industry groups; US export management companies; and training companies focused on international topics. Although some of the people might overlap at the events, each organization has a different focus and provides different resources.

BOOKS, PODCASTS, WEBSITES

Somewhere, someone already struggled with the same issue a new exporter might encounter. Luckily, accessing information or finding a resource to answer your questions is easier than ever.

For example, at Rapport International, we strive to educate people on multilingual communications, translation, interpreting, global marketing, and cultural adaptation. As you know, we host guests on the *Global Marketing Show* (found on all your favorite podcast listening apps!) to talk about their real-life experiences. In addition, our prior book is a how-to book on starting global marketing – *The Language of Global Marketing*, and at www.RapportTranslations.com you will find a full learning resource center with information to help with multilingual communications and cross-border trade. Like Rapport International, many other service providers offer information to help clients learn what to expect.

SERVICE PROVIDERS

Service providers offer insight, resources, and a supportive network. Call on a trusted partner in any of the areas listed below to get advice and recommendations for other high-quality providers. The best vendors participate in networking organizations or partner with other providers to fully service all their clients' needs.

- Language services providers (LSPs) or translation agencies – start with us at Rapport International!
- Payment companies, e.g., Zonos and Corpay

- Shipping and logistics providers
- Insurance companies
- Tax, legal, and regulatory services
- Trade consultants
- Incubators
- Professional employer organizations (PEOs), otherwise known as employee leasing companies, for hiring and managing international employees
- Banks, such as the Export-Import Bank of the United States (EXIM), the official export credit agency of the US

If you're still not convinced, here is sage advice from an export consultant: "Always be thinking about exporting! The advantages are huge – you offset a domestic home market, find new customers, get unexpected new ideas, discover product improvements, employ more people, and beat your competitors!"

FINAL KEY POINTS TO REMEMBER:

- Access the many resources that exist for companies that want to export.
- Track your success so you can see that you enjoy more opportunities and higher revenues than your non-exporting competition.
- Reach out to trade advisors, vendors, and service providers and ask for help. It is a hugely supportive network!

Hear Wendy's full podcast episode at

- https://www.rapporttranslations.com/the-global-marketing-show/untapped-global-growth-export

CHAPTER 21

SUCCESS IS ATTAINABLE!

"The stories about successful exporters are inspiring!"

—Hannah Feldman Pentz, Global Marketing Expert

A fter publishing *The Language of Global Marketing* to address frequently asked questions from our clients and outline a way to "translate domestic strategies into international sales and profits," we realized that guests of the *Global Marketing Show* shared invaluable advice and real-life experience not captured before. We wanted to highlight their knowledge, share stories of their global ventures and the challenges they overcame, as well as extend their advice for the roughly 37% of US companies that "don't know where to start." With so many guests to choose from, each with their own unique perspective and experiences, it was difficult to narrow down what to share! Our goal became to take you, our reader, on a journey and touch upon some common themes from our clients and network of global service providers.

In our work at Rapport International, where we provide high-quality written translation and spoken interpreting services, we encounter and support the successes of many companies that export.

Here are a few examples:

1. Numberall Manufacturing Company's Vice President explained, *"Our exports grew from about 7% of revenues before we translated to*

about 15% after we translated our website. We see a spike of visitors whenever we post a popular Spanish blog."

2. Conitex Sonoco's Digital Marketing Manager noted, *"Since adding translation, our website sessions have increased by 85% in Spanish-speaking countries, 158% in Indonesia, and 22% in China."*

3. The Gerson Company's Senior Graphic Designer shared, *"Due to our highly regulated products, Gerson could not sell internationally without translations of our instructions for use and packaging. Over the past few years, we have signed seven new international distributors and three new international client contracts. This has supported our revenue growth of over 20%."*

4. Ranfac's COO explained, *"We can now do business in Europe with Rapport International's translation for the CE Mark requirements. Without their translation we could not export to Europe. Our exports have grown by 8% in 2021 and faster than that prior to Covid. Plus, we opened in two new markets (Sri Lanka and the Middle East) and signed 8-10 new meaningful contracts in the last four years. Exporting is now 25% of our total business."*

We hope that the stories we shared here, and the accomplishments of the many companies we supported on their global journeys, will be inspiring and encouraging as you travel on your own global paths. Remember, there are **resources to help you, international consumers that want your product, and exporting benefits to foster prosperity.**

Check out the next and last chapter to view the Bonus Materials and Special Offers to access resources to support your journey.

Have Fun and Keep Growing!

CHAPTER 22

BONUS MATERIALS AND SPECIAL OFFERS

BONUS MATERIAL

In this book we captured highlights of our guests' stories and unfortunately had to remove other important information in order to keep the book a reasonable length. Yet, all is not lost! We gathered this helpful information into "Bonus Material" to support your global journey. You can find:

- Contacts at each USEAC for export assistance
- Books and podcasts we find helpful
- Website content for deeper insights
- Lists of providers we recommend
- Organizations, groups, and communities to build global networks
- Federal and state resources
- And much, much more!

Visit https://www.rapporttranslations.com/bonus-materials to access your complimentary information.

SPECIAL OFFERS

Service providers have deep experience and offer helpful advice to exporters. Also, they have connections in the global trade community from supporting exporters and working with other partners. For the highest chance of success, build a good support system and lean on your service providers for ideas, introductions, and inspiration.

These Special Offers are for valuable services from people we met while serving on the District Export Council, attending global trade shows, participating in global trade communities, listening to feedback from trade experts, and from years of being connected. The list is continually growing and changing.

- Keep the link marked as a favorite so you can find it when you need it.

- Please, share your feedback on any Special Offer you try or introduce us to other experts that you like working with. It's all about the network!

- Visit https://www.rapporttranslations.com/special-offers to access your Special Offers.

Please see this book as an invitation to connect and share your journey with us:

Wendy MacKenzie Pease

- https://www.linkedin.com/in/wendypease/
- wmpease@RapportTranslations.com
- +1 978-443-2540 x101

Hannah Feldman Pentz

- https://www.linkedin.com/in/hannah-feldman-pentz-2297aa22/

ENDNOTES

ENDNOTES

1   https://www.trade.gov/why-export

2   https://www.census.gov/data/tables/2019/econ/abs/2019-abs-exporting-firms.html

3   https://ustr.gov/issue-areas/small-business#:~:text=Small%20businesses%20which%20export%20grow,both%20direct%20and%20indirect%20exports

4   https://www.rapporttranslations.com/the-global-marketing-show

5   https://lightwaydigital.com

6   https://www.trade.gov/strategic-reasons-export

7   https://vispera.co

8   https://www.voltus.co

9   https://www.sonoco.com/na

10   http://www.modelfront.com

11   https://aclanthology.org/www.mt-archive.info/10/Hutchins-2014.pdf

12   http://www.tellcarole.com/

13   https://GlobalHola.com

14 https://www.hofstede-insights.com/country-comparison-tool

15 Ibid

16 Ibid

17 Ibid

18 https://www.globalsalesmentor.com

19 https://csa-research.com/Featured-Content/For-Global-Enterprises/
Global-Growth/CRWB-Series/CRWB-B2C

20 https://www.blackbox.com/en-us

21 https://www.tuvsud.com/en

22 https://brooksmadegourmetfoods.com/

23 Can't Read, Won't Buy - B2C, July 2020, CSA Research, Donald
A. DePalma and Paul O'Mara

24 https://b2linked.com

25 http://www.sparksworldwide.com/

26 US Department of Commerce, https://www.trade.gov/why-
export#:~:text=Exporting%20can%20be%20profitable%20
for,service%2C%20and%20sound%20business%20practices.

27 https://www.linkedin.com/in/daniweinstein/

28 https://www.edmarshconsulting.com/

29 https://csa-research.com/Featured-Content/For-Global-Enterprises/
Localization-Maturity-Assessment

30 www.RapportTranslations.com

31 https://advocacy.sba.gov/wp-content/uploads/2024/03/Issue-Brief-
No.-19-Small-Business-Exports.pdf

32 https://economictimes.indiatimes.com/small-biz/sme-sector/
small-online-businesses-outperform-traditional-traders-with-
93-export-rate-in-18-countries-report/articleshow/101511244.
cms?from=mdr#google_vignette

ACKNOWLEDGMENTS

This book would not have been possible without the generosity of our podcast guests, our colleagues, editors, and families.

Thank you to the podcast guests for sharing their stories – without you, there would be no book (in order of appearance in the book): Omar Menashe, Aytul Ercil, Brittany Cooper Kingdon, Stephanie Hendricks, John Jove, Michelle Safrit, Adam Bittlingmayer, Carole Copeland Thomas, Nick Canfield, Zach Selch, Randi Roger, Andrew Jason, Liz Fendt, Walter Brooks, Viveka Von Rosen, Babs Ryan, Dani Weinstein, Ed Marsh, and Patrick Nunes.

Thank you to all the other guests of the podcast who opened up about their experiences. We've learned so much from you!

Thank you to Lisa Rea for launching the podcast and for editing the book.

Thank you to Wendy Miller for your edits and thoughts on exclamation points!

Thank you to Haley Simpkiss for your attention to detail and knowledge of grammar and punctuation. We learned so much from you!

Thank you to Linda Spooner for being who you are.

Thank you to all our clients who make life possible!

ABOUT THE AUTHORS

WENDY MACKENZIE PEASE

Wendy MacKenzie Pease is the Owner and President of Rapport International, a language services company that provides high-quality, culturally adapted translation and interpretation services with a specialty in global marketing, legal documents, employee communications, and medical/life sciences. Throughout her career, she has worked with hundreds of companies to help them communicate across more than 200 languages and cultures.

Wendy is a frequent speaker, writer, blogger, trainer, advisor, and master networker. She's the author of the book *The Language of Global Marketing* and the host of the *Global Marketing Show* podcast, which features experts on opportunities and challenges in increasing multilingual lead gen and revenue.

Wendy's passionate about connecting people across languages and cultures. She has lived in Mexico, Taiwan, and the Philippines, where she fell in love with differing cultures and came to understand that we are all human, no matter the language we speak. Learn more at https://www.rapporttranslations.com/wendy-pease

HANNAH FELDMAN PENTZ

Hannah Feldman Pentz, an experienced marketing and communications professional, has created and implemented strategic communication plans for leading global management consultancies, business-to-business organizations, and non-profits.

By helping define and launch marketing strategies, brand messaging, and public relations campaigns, she has helped organizations achieve and maintain their market goals.

An incredible junior year abroad experience initiated her love for travel. She loves to travel and learn about other people and cultures, especially with her family.

www.ingramcontent.com/pod-product-compliance
Lightning Source LLC
Chambersburg PA
CBHW070331130626
46556CB00007B/2804